TEACHER'S PET PUBLICATIONS

PUZZLE PACK
for
The River

based on the book by
Gary Paulsen

Written by
William T. Collins

© 2005 Teacher's Pet Publications
All Rights Reserved

The materials in this packet are copyrighted
by Teacher's Pet Publications, Inc.

These pages may be duplicated by the purchaser
for use in the purchaser's own classroom.

Copying any of these materials and distributing them
for any other purpose is a violation of the copyright laws.

© 2005 Teacher's Pet Publications, Inc.
www.tpet.com

## INTRODUCTION
If you already own the LitPlan for this title, this Puzzle Pack will refresh your Unit Resource Materials and Vocabulary Resource Materials sections plus give you additional materials you can substitute into the tests. If you do not already have a complete LitPlan, these pages will give you some supplemental materials to use with your own plan. There are two main groups of materials: one set for unit words (such as characters' names, symbols, places, etc.) and one set for vocabulary words associated with the book.

## WORD LIST
There is a word list for both the unit words and the vocabulary words. These lists show you which words are being used in the materials and the clues or definitions being used for those words. You may want to give students a word list with clues/definitions to help them, or you may want students to only have a word list (without clues/definitions) if you want them to work a little harder. Both are available for duplication. The word lists can also be your "calling key" for the bingo games.

## FILL IN THE BLANK AND MATCHING
There are 4 each of the fill in the blank and matching worksheets for both the unit and vocabulary words. These pages can be used either as extra worksheets for students or as objective parts of a unit test. They can be done individually if students need extra help or as a whole class activity to review the material covered.

## MAGIC SQUARES
The magic squares not only reinforce the material covered but also work on reasoning and math skills. Many teachers have told us that their students really enjoy doing these!

## WORD SEARCH PUZZLES
The word search words go in all directions, as indicated on your answer keys. Two of the word search puzzles have the clues listed rather than the words. This makes the puzzle a little more difficult, but it reinforces the material better. Two word search puzzles have words only for students who find the clue puzzles too difficult.

## CROSSWORD PUZZLES
Both unit and vocabulary word sections have 4 crossword puzzles.

## BINGO CARDS
There are 32 individual bingo cards for the unit words and 32 individual bingo cards for the vocabulary words. You can use your word list as a "call list," calling the words at random and marking them off of your list as you go, or you could use the flash cards by cutting them apart and drawing the words at random from a hat (or box or whatever). To make a better review, you might ask for the definition and spelling of each word as you call it out–or you could call out the definitions and have students tell you the words they need to look for on the puzzle.

## JUGGLE LETTERS
The vocabulary juggle letter game is intended to help students learn the spellings of the words. One sheet has the definitions listed on it as an extra help for students who need it or to reinforce the definitions if you choose to do so.

## FLASH CARDS
We've included a set of vocabulary flash cards you can duplicate, cut, and fold for your students. Some teachers make a few sets for general use by the class; others make a set for each student. Some teachers duplicate them for each student and have the students cut & fold their own. You can cut out just the words and put them in a hat, have each student pick out one word and write the definition and a sentence for that word. Students then swap words and papers, with the next student adding a sentence of his own under the last one. You can have students swap as many times as you like. Each time the student will read the sentences written prior to his own and then add a sentence. You can cut out the words and definitions separately and play "I Have; Who Has?" Each student in the room draws a word and definition. The first student says, "I have (the name of the word). Who has the definition?" The student with the definition reads it then says, "I have (the name of the vocabulary word she has). Who has the definition?" The round continues until all words and definitions have been given.

### The River Word List

| No. | Word | Clue/Definition |
|---|---|---|
| 1. | BALLARD | Erik ____; government survival instructor |
| 2. | BEAVERS | They cut the trees that Brian used for the raft. |
| 3. | BIRCH | ____bark; used for food containers |
| 4. | BOUGHS | Pine ____; used for their beds |
| 5. | BRANNOCK | Name of trading post |
| 6. | BRIAN | Two-time wilderness survivor |
| 7. | BRIEFCASE | Contained the map, notebooks, and radio |
| 8. | CANOE | Gift to Brian from Derek |
| 9. | CHUTE | Dangerous, rocky water |
| 10. | COMA | Derek's medical state |
| 11. | COOK | Brian's new hobby after first time in the wilderness |
| 12. | COUNSELOR | Thought Brian was mentally injured |
| 13. | DEBORAH | ____McKenzie; Brian's girlfriend |
| 14. | ETHICS | Derek admired Brian's |
| 15. | FIFTEEN | Brian's age during the trip |
| 16. | FIRE | They didn't have one the first night. |
| 17. | FLINT | Needed to make a fire |
| 18. | FOOD | It was 'everything' in the wild, according to Brian. |
| 19. | GRUBWORMS | Possible food |
| 20. | HOLTZER | Derek ____; psychologist who went with Brian |
| 21. | HUNGER | Brian's worst problem during The Time |
| 22. | JACKET | Brian used it to make strips. |
| 23. | KATIE | ____ONE; radio station code name |
| 24. | KNIVES | Their only tools |
| 25. | LIGHTNING | Caused the problems on the trip |
| 26. | MANNERLY | Bill____ said the government wanted Brian to teach them. |
| 27. | MAP | Showed the way to the trading post |
| 28. | MOSQUITOES | Attacked the first night |
| 29. | NECKTIE | Name of the river |
| 30. | PAULSEN | Author |
| 31. | POPLAR | Trees used for the raft |
| 32. | RADIO | Left behind on trip down the river |
| 33. | RAFT | Name of the canoe |
| 34. | RASPBERRIES | First Food |
| 35. | ROBESON | Mr. ____ was about to get married. |
| 36. | SEVEN | Months after trip when Brian received Derek's gift |
| 37. | SIX | Months for Derek to recover |
| 38. | SURVIVAL | Kind of gear left behind in the plane |
| 39. | TENSION | The first part of the trip lacked it. |
| 40. | TIME | The ____; Brian's name for his first wilderness experience |
| 41. | TWELVE | Pounds Brian lost |
| 42. | TWO | Katie ____; Brian and Derek's code name |
| 43. | WOOD | Brian said there could never be too much of it. |

The River Fill In The Blanks 1

_____  1. Author
_____  2. First Food
_____  3. They didn't have one the first night.
_____  4. Their only tools
_____  5. Brian's worst problem during The Time
_____  6. Name of the river
_____  7. Dangerous, rocky water
_____  8. Brian said there could never be too much of it.
_____  9. Brian's age during the trip
_____ 10. Mr. ____ was about to get married.
_____ 11. Contained the map, notebooks, and radio
_____ 12. Brian's new hobby after first time in the wilderness
_____ 13. Derek admired Brian's
_____ 14. Derek ____; psychologist who went with Brian
_____ 15. Possible food
_____ 16. ____bark; used for food containers
_____ 17. Gift to Brian from Derek
_____ 18. Bill____ said the government wanted Brian to teach them.
_____ 19. Months after trip when Brian received Derek's gift
_____ 20. Attacked the first night

The River Fill In The Blanks 1 Answer Key

| PAULSEN | 1. Author |
| RASPBERRIES | 2. First Food |
| FIRE | 3. They didn't have one the first night. |
| KNIVES | 4. Their only tools |
| HUNGER | 5. Brian's worst problem during The Time |
| NECKTIE | 6. Name of the river |
| CHUTE | 7. Dangerous, rocky water |
| WOOD | 8. Brian said there could never be too much of it. |
| FIFTEEN | 9. Brian's age during the trip |
| ROBESON | 10. Mr. ____ was about to get married. |
| BRIEFCASE | 11. Contained the map, notebooks, and radio |
| COOK | 12. Brian's new hobby after first time in the wilderness |
| ETHICS | 13. Derek admired Brian's |
| HOLTZER | 14. Derek ____; psychologist who went with Brian |
| GRUBWORMS | 15. Possible food |
| BIRCH | 16. ____bark; used for food containers |
| CANOE | 17. Gift to Brian from Derek |
| MANNERLY | 18. Bill____ said the government wanted Brian to teach them. |
| SEVEN | 19. Months after trip when Brian received Derek's gift |
| MOSQUITOES | 20. Attacked the first night |

The River Fill In The Blanks 2

_____  1. Name of the canoe

_____  2. Name of the river

_____  3. Derek admired Brian's

_____  4. Brian used it to make strips.

_____  5. The ____; Brian's name for his first wilderness experience

_____  6. Brian said there could never be too much of it.

_____  7. Author

_____  8. It was 'everything' in the wild, according to Brian.

_____  9. Two-time wilderness survivor

_____  10. First Food

_____  11. ____McKenzie; Brian's girlfriend

_____  12. Showed the way to the trading post

_____  13. Brian's age during the trip

_____  14. They cut the trees that Brian used for the raft.

_____  15. Possible food

_____  16. Bill____ said the government wanted Brian to teach them.

_____  17. Mr. ____ was about to get married.

_____  18. Erik ____; government survival instructor

_____  19. Months after trip when Brian received Derek's gift

_____  20. Contained the map, notebooks, and radio

The River Fill In The Blanks 2 Answer Key

| | |
|---|---|
| RAFT | 1. Name of the canoe |
| NECKTIE | 2. Name of the river |
| ETHICS | 3. Derek admired Brian's |
| JACKET | 4. Brian used it to make strips. |
| TIME | 5. The ____; Brian's name for his first wilderness experience |
| WOOD | 6. Brian said there could never be too much of it. |
| PAULSEN | 7. Author |
| FOOD | 8. It was 'everything' in the wild, according to Brian. |
| BRIAN | 9. Two-time wilderness survivor |
| RASPBERRIES | 10. First Food |
| DEBORAH | 11. ____McKenzie; Brian's girlfriend |
| MAP | 12. Showed the way to the trading post |
| FIFTEEN | 13. Brian's age during the trip |
| BEAVERS | 14. They cut the trees that Brian used for the raft. |
| GRUBWORMS | 15. Possible food |
| MANNERLY | 16. Bill____ said the government wanted Brian to teach them. |
| ROBESON | 17. Mr. ____ was about to get married. |
| BALLARD | 18. Erik ____; government survival instructor |
| SEVEN | 19. Months after trip when Brian received Derek's gift |
| BRIEFCASE | 20. Contained the map, notebooks, and radio |

The River Fill In The Blanks 3

_____
_____
_____
_____
_____
_____
_____
_____
_____
_____
_____
_____
_____
_____
_____
_____
_____
_____
_____
_____

1. ____bark; used for food containers
2. Derek admired Brian's
3. Their only tools
4. Author
5. Two-time wilderness survivor
6. They didn't have one the first night.
7. Brian used it to make strips.
8. Trees used for the raft
9. Brian's worst problem during The Time
10. Months after trip when Brian received Derek's gift
11. Months for Derek to recover
12. The ____; Brian's name for his first wilderness experience
13. Pine ____; used for their beds
14. Name of the canoe
15. First Food
16. Katie ____; Brian and Derek's code name
17. Showed the way to the trading post
18. Erik ____; government survival instructor
19. They cut the trees that Brian used for the raft.
20. Brian's new hobby after first time in the wilderness

The River Fill In The Blanks 3 Answer Key

| | |
|---|---|
| BIRCH | 1. ____bark; used for food containers |
| ETHICS | 2. Derek admired Brian's |
| KNIVES | 3. Their only tools |
| PAULSEN | 4. Author |
| BRIAN | 5. Two-time wilderness survivor |
| FIRE | 6. They didn't have one the first night. |
| JACKET | 7. Brian used it to make strips. |
| POPLAR | 8. Trees used for the raft |
| HUNGER | 9. Brian's worst problem during The Time |
| SEVEN | 10. Months after trip when Brian received Derek's gift |
| SIX | 11. Months for Derek to recover |
| TIME | 12. The ____; Brian's name for his first wilderness experience |
| BOUGHS | 13. Pine ____; used for their beds |
| RAFT | 14. Name of the canoe |
| RASPBERRIES | 15. First Food |
| TWO | 16. Katie ____; Brian and Derek's code name |
| MAP | 17. Showed the way to the trading post |
| BALLARD | 18. Erik ____; government survival instructor |
| BEAVERS | 19. They cut the trees that Brian used for the raft. |
| COOK | 20. Brian's new hobby after first time in the wilderness |

# The River Fill In The Blanks 4

_____  1. Contained the map, notebooks, and radio

_____  2. Trees used for the raft

_____  3. Months for Derek to recover

_____  4. ____McKenzie; Brian's girlfriend

_____  5. Derek admired Brian's

_____  6. Erik ____; government survival instructor

_____  7. Brian said there could never be too much of it.

_____  8. Kind of gear left behind in the plane

_____  9. Their only tools

_____  10. Brian used it to make strips.

_____  11. Katie ____; Brian and Derek's code name

_____  12. Gift to Brian from Derek

_____  13. Brian's age during the trip

_____  14. Attacked the first night

_____  15. Dangerous, rocky water

_____  16. Left behind on trip down the river

_____  17. Author

_____  18. Possible food

_____  19. Derek's medical state

_____  20. The ____; Brian's name for his first wilderness experience

The River Fill In The Blanks 4 Answer Key

| | |
|---|---|
| BRIEFCASE | 1. Contained the map, notebooks, and radio |
| POPLAR | 2. Trees used for the raft |
| SIX | 3. Months for Derek to recover |
| DEBORAH | 4. ____McKenzie; Brian's girlfriend |
| ETHICS | 5. Derek admired Brian's |
| BALLARD | 6. Erik ____; government survival instructor |
| WOOD | 7. Brian said there could never be too much of it. |
| SURVIVAL | 8. Kind of gear left behind in the plane |
| KNIVES | 9. Their only tools |
| JACKET | 10. Brian used it to make strips. |
| TWO | 11. Katie ____; Brian and Derek's code name |
| CANOE | 12. Gift to Brian from Derek |
| FIFTEEN | 13. Brian's age during the trip |
| MOSQUITOES | 14. Attacked the first night |
| CHUTE | 15. Dangerous, rocky water |
| RADIO | 16. Left behind on trip down the river |
| PAULSEN | 17. Author |
| GRUBWORMS | 18. Possible food |
| COMA | 19. Derek's medical state |
| TIME | 20. The ____; Brian's name for his first wilderness experience |

The River Matching 1

___ 1. RADIO             A. First Food
___ 2. JACKET            B. Showed the way to the trading post
___ 3. NECKTIE           C. Needed to make a fire
___ 4. SURVIVAL          D. Brian's age during the trip
___ 5. COMA              E. ____ONE; radio station code name
___ 6. RAFT              F. Brian used it to make strips.
___ 7. FIRE              G. They didn't have one the first night.
___ 8. ETHICS            H. Derek admired Brian's
___ 9. TENSION           I. Left behind on trip down the river
___10. MAP               J. Trees used for the raft
___11. SIX               K. Kind of gear left behind in the plane
___12. MANNERLY          L. Bill____ said the government wanted Brian to teach them.
___13. DEBORAH           M. Name of the river
___14. BRIEFCASE         N. Months for Derek to recover
___15. BALLARD           O. Gift to Brian from Derek
___16. FIFTEEN           P. ____bark; used for food containers
___17. CHUTE             Q. Pounds Brian lost
___18. RASPBERRIES       R. Dangerous, rocky water
___19. FLINT             S. Name of the canoe
___20. POPLAR            T. ____McKenzie; Brian's girlfriend
___21. BIRCH             U. Brian said there could never be too much of it.
___22. TWELVE            V. The first part of the trip lacked it.
___23. CANOE             W. Contained the map, notebooks, and radio
___24. WOOD              X. Erik ____; government survival instructor
___25. KATIE             Y. Derek's medical state

The River Matching 1 Answer Key

| | | | |
|---|---|---|---|
| I - 1. RADIO | | A. | First Food |
| F - 2. JACKET | | B. | Showed the way to the trading post |
| M - 3. NECKTIE | | C. | Needed to make a fire |
| K - 4. SURVIVAL | | D. | Brian's age during the trip |
| Y - 5. COMA | | E. | ____ONE; radio station code name |
| S - 6. RAFT | | F. | Brian used it to make strips. |
| G - 7. FIRE | | G. | They didn't have one the first night. |
| H - 8. ETHICS | | H. | Derek admired Brian's |
| V - 9. TENSION | | I. | Left behind on trip down the river |
| B - 10. MAP | | J. | Trees used for the raft |
| N - 11. SIX | | K. | Kind of gear left behind in the plane |
| L - 12. MANNERLY | | L. | Bill____ said the government wanted Brian to teach them. |
| T - 13. DEBORAH | | M. | Name of the river |
| W - 14. BRIEFCASE | | N. | Months for Derek to recover |
| X - 15. BALLARD | | O. | Gift to Brian from Derek |
| D - 16. FIFTEEN | | P. | ____bark; used for food containers |
| R - 17. CHUTE | | Q. | Pounds Brian lost |
| A - 18. RASPBERRIES | | R. | Dangerous, rocky water |
| C - 19. FLINT | | S. | Name of the canoe |
| J - 20. POPLAR | | T. | ____McKenzie; Brian's girlfriend |
| P - 21. BIRCH | | U. | Brian said there could never be too much of it. |
| Q - 22. TWELVE | | V. | The first part of the trip lacked it. |
| O - 23. CANOE | | W. | Contained the map, notebooks, and radio |
| U - 24. WOOD | | X. | Erik ____; government survival instructor |
| E - 25. KATIE | | Y. | Derek's medical state |

Copyrighted

The River Matching 2

___ 1. KNIVES          A. Caused the problems on the trip
___ 2. PAULSEN         B. ____McKenzie; Brian's girlfriend
___ 3. CANOE           C. Attacked the first night
___ 4. BOUGHS          D. Pine ____; used for their beds
___ 5. FIRE            E. They didn't have one the first night.
___ 6. FLINT           F. Thought Brian was mentally injured
___ 7. BRIAN           G. Their only tools
___ 8. BALLARD         H. Contained the map, notebooks, and radio
___ 9. SEVEN           I. Brian's worst problem during The Time
___10. TWO             J. Bill____ said the government wanted Brian to teach them.
___11. ETHICS          K. Months after trip when Brian received Derek's gift
___12. MOSQUITOES      L. Brian's new hobby after first time in the wilderness
___13. HUNGER          M. ____bark; used for food containers
___14. COOK            N. Needed to make a fire
___15. DEBORAH         O. Name of trading post
___16. LIGHTNING       P. Derek admired Brian's
___17. BRANNOCK        Q. Gift to Brian from Derek
___18. TIME            R. Name of the canoe
___19. RAFT            S. Brian said there could never be too much of it.
___20. BIRCH           T. Author
___21. BRIEFCASE       U. Erik ____; government survival instructor
___22. COUNSELOR       V. Two-time wilderness survivor
___23. KATIE           W. The ____; Brian's name for his first wilderness experience
___24. MANNERLY        X. ____ONE; radio station code name
___25. WOOD            Y. Katie ____; Brian and Derek's code name

# The River Matching 2 Answer Key

G - 1. KNIVES   A. Caused the problems on the trip
T - 2. PAULSEN   B. ____McKenzie; Brian's girlfriend
Q - 3. CANOE   C. Attacked the first night
D - 4. BOUGHS   D. Pine ____; used for their beds
E - 5. FIRE   E. They didn't have one the first night.
N - 6. FLINT   F. Thought Brian was mentally injured
V - 7. BRIAN   G. Their only tools
U - 8. BALLARD   H. Contained the map, notebooks, and radio
K - 9. SEVEN   I. Brian's worst problem during The Time
Y - 10. TWO   J. Bill____ said the government wanted Brian to teach them.
P - 11. ETHICS   K. Months after trip when Brian received Derek's gift
C - 12. MOSQUITOES   L. Brian's new hobby after first time in the wilderness
I - 13. HUNGER   M. ____bark; used for food containers
L - 14. COOK   N. Needed to make a fire
B - 15. DEBORAH   O. Name of trading post
A - 16. LIGHTNING   P. Derek admired Brian's
O - 17. BRANNOCK   Q. Gift to Brian from Derek
W - 18. TIME   R. Name of the canoe
R - 19. RAFT   S. Brian said there could never be too much of it.
M - 20. BIRCH   T. Author
H - 21. BRIEFCASE   U. Erik ____; government survival instructor
F - 22. COUNSELOR   V. Two-time wilderness survivor
X - 23. KATIE   W. The ____; Brian's name for his first wilderness experience
J - 24. MANNERLY   X. ____ONE; radio station code name
S - 25. WOOD   Y. Katie ____; Brian and Derek's code name

The River Matching 3

___ 1. MANNERLY         A. Left behind on trip down the river
___ 2. ROBESON          B. Months for Derek to recover
___ 3. MOSQUITOES       C. Derek ____; psychologist who went with Brian
___ 4. SURVIVAL         D. Brian said there could never be too much of it.
___ 5. KATIE            E. Gift to Brian from Derek
___ 6. GRUBWORMS        F. Possible food
___ 7. ETHICS           G. ____ONE; radio station code name
___ 8. BEAVERS          H. Mr. ____ was about to get married.
___ 9. LIGHTNING        I. They didn't have one the first night.
___10. TIME             J. It was 'everything' in the wild, according to Brian.
___11. RADIO            K. The first part of the trip lacked it.
___12. TWO              L. Trees used for the raft
___13. BALLARD          M. Erik ____; government survival instructor
___14. FOOD             N. ____McKenzie; Brian's girlfriend
___15. DEBORAH          O. Katie ____; Brian and Derek's code name
___16. POPLAR           P. The ____; Brian's name for his first wilderness experience
___17. TWELVE           Q. They cut the trees that Brian used for the raft.
___18. TENSION          R. Caused the problems on the trip
___19. COMA             S. Attacked the first night
___20. SIX              T. Pounds Brian lost
___21. FIRE             U. Kind of gear left behind in the plane
___22. RAFT             V. Derek's medical state
___23. CANOE            W. Name of the canoe
___24. WOOD             X. Bill____ said the government wanted Brian to teach them.
___25. HOLTZER          Y. Derek admired Brian's

The River Matching 3 Answer Key

| | | |
|---|---|---|
| X - 1. | MANNERLY | A. Left behind on trip down the river |
| H - 2. | ROBESON | B. Months for Derek to recover |
| S - 3. | MOSQUITOES | C. Derek ____; psychologist who went with Brian |
| U - 4. | SURVIVAL | D. Brian said there could never be too much of it. |
| G - 5. | KATIE | E. Gift to Brian from Derek |
| F - 6. | GRUBWORMS | F. Possible food |
| Y - 7. | ETHICS | G. ____ONE; radio station code name |
| Q - 8. | BEAVERS | H. Mr. ____ was about to get married. |
| R - 9. | LIGHTNING | I. They didn't have one the first night. |
| P - 10. | TIME | J. It was 'everything' in the wild, according to Brian. |
| A - 11. | RADIO | K. The first part of the trip lacked it. |
| O - 12. | TWO | L. Trees used for the raft |
| M - 13. | BALLARD | M. Erik ____; government survival instructor |
| J - 14. | FOOD | N. ____McKenzie; Brian's girlfriend |
| N - 15. | DEBORAH | O. Katie ____; Brian and Derek's code name |
| L - 16. | POPLAR | P. The ____; Brian's name for his first wilderness experience |
| T - 17. | TWELVE | Q. They cut the trees that Brian used for the raft. |
| K - 18. | TENSION | R. Caused the problems on the trip |
| V - 19. | COMA | S. Attacked the first night |
| B - 20. | SIX | T. Pounds Brian lost |
| I - 21. | FIRE | U. Kind of gear left behind in the plane |
| W - 22. | RAFT | V. Derek's medical state |
| E - 23. | CANOE | W. Name of the canoe |
| D - 24. | WOOD | X. Bill____ said the government wanted Brian to teach them. |
| C - 25. | HOLTZER | Y. Derek admired Brian's |

The River Matching 4

___ 1. BRANNOCK          A. Two-time wilderness survivor
___ 2. HOLTZER           B. Needed to make a fire
___ 3. BIRCH             C. Trees used for the raft
___ 4. FLINT             D. Erik ____; government survival instructor
___ 5. NECKTIE           E. Pounds Brian lost
___ 6. SIX               F. Mr. ____ was about to get married.
___ 7. TIME              G. The ____; Brian's name for his first wilderness experience
___ 8. MAP               H. Contained the map, notebooks, and radio
___ 9. TWELVE            I. Name of the river
___10. BALLARD           J. ____bark; used for food containers
___11. LIGHTNING         K. Months for Derek to recover
___12. COUNSELOR         L. ____ONE; radio station code name
___13. BRIEFCASE         M. Dangerous, rocky water
___14. POPLAR            N. Brian's worst problem during The Time
___15. KATIE             O. Brian said there could never be too much of it.
___16. MOSQUITOES        P. Thought Brian was mentally injured
___17. FIRE              Q. Brian used it to make strips.
___18. ROBESON           R. Pine ____; used for their beds
___19. HUNGER            S. Name of trading post
___20. BOUGHS            T. Attacked the first night
___21. CHUTE             U. Derek ____; psychologist who went with Brian
___22. JACKET            V. The first part of the trip lacked it.
___23. WOOD              W. Showed the way to the trading post
___24. BRIAN             X. Caused the problems on the trip
___25. TENSION           Y. They didn't have one the first night.

The River Matching 4 Answer Key

S - 1. BRANNOCK          A. Two-time wilderness survivor
U - 2. HOLTZER           B. Needed to make a fire
J - 3. BIRCH             C. Trees used for the raft
B - 4. FLINT             D. Erik ____; government survival instructor
I - 5. NECKTIE           E. Pounds Brian lost
K - 6. SIX               F. Mr. ____ was about to get married.
G - 7. TIME              G. The ____; Brian's name for his first wilderness experience
W - 8. MAP               H. Contained the map, notebooks, and radio
E - 9. TWELVE            I. Name of the river
D - 10. BALLARD          J. ____bark; used for food containers
X - 11. LIGHTNING        K. Months for Derek to recover
P - 12. COUNSELOR        L. ____ONE; radio station code name
H - 13. BRIEFCASE        M. Dangerous, rocky water
C - 14. POPLAR           N. Brian's worst problem during The Time
L - 15. KATIE            O. Brian said there could never be too much of it.
T - 16. MOSQUITOES       P. Thought Brian was mentally injured
Y - 17. FIRE             Q. Brian used it to make strips.
F - 18. ROBESON          R. Pine ____; used for their beds
N - 19. HUNGER           S. Name of trading post
R - 20. BOUGHS           T. Attacked the first night
M - 21. CHUTE            U. Derek ____; psychologist who went with Brian
Q - 22. JACKET           V. The first part of the trip lacked it.
O - 23. WOOD             W. Showed the way to the trading post
A - 24. BRIAN            X. Caused the problems on the trip
V - 25. TENSION          Y. They didn't have one the first night.

The River Magic Squares 1

Match the definition with the vocabulary word. Put your answers in the magic squares below. When your answers are correct, all columns and rows will add to the same number.

A. HUNGER
B. BRANNOCK
C. BRIEFCASE
D. MANNERLY
E. TENSION
F. KATIE
G. FOOD
H. FIRE
I. KNIVES
J. ROBESON
K. RAFT
L. BIRCH
M. CANOE
N. POPLAR
O. TWELVE
P. COOK

1. Gift to Brian from Derek
2. ____ONE; radio station code name
3. They didn't have one the first night.
4. Pounds Brian lost
5. ____bark; used for food containers
6. Contained the map, notebooks, and radio
7. Brian's worst problem during The Time
8. Mr. ____ was about to get married.
9. Name of the canoe
10. Bill____ said the government wanted Brian to teach them.
11. Name of trading post
12. Their only tools
13. Trees used for the raft
14. The first part of the trip lacked it.
15. It was 'everything' in the wild, according to Brian.
16. Brian's new hobby after first time in the wilderness

| A= | B= | C= | D= |
|---|---|---|---|
| E= | F= | G= | H= |
| I= | J= | K= | L= |
| M= | N= | O= | P= |

The River Magic Squares 1 Answer Key

Match the definition with the vocabulary word. Put your answers in the magic squares below. When your answers are correct, all columns and rows will add to the same number.

A. HUNGER
B. BRANNOCK
C. BRIEFCASE
D. MANNERLY
E. TENSION
F. KATIE
G. FOOD
H. FIRE
I. KNIVES
J. ROBESON
K. RAFT
L. BIRCH
M. CANOE
N. POPLAR
O. TWELVE
P. COOK

1. Gift to Brian from Derek
2. ____ONE; radio station code name
3. They didn't have one the first night.
4. Pounds Brian lost
5. ____bark; used for food containers
6. Contained the map, notebooks, and radio
7. Brian's worst problem during The Time
8. Mr. ____ was about to get married.
9. Name of the canoe
10. Bill____ said the government wanted Brian to teach them.
11. Name of trading post
12. Their only tools
13. Trees used for the raft
14. The first part of the trip lacked it.
15. It was 'everything' in the wild, according to Brian.
16. Brian's new hobby after first time in the wilderness

| A=7 | B=11 | C=6 | D=10 |
| --- | --- | --- | --- |
| E=14 | F=2 | G=15 | H=3 |
| I=12 | J=8 | K=9 | L=5 |
| M=1 | N=13 | O=4 | P=16 |

The River Magic Squares 2

Match the definition with the vocabulary word. Put your answers in the magic squares below. When your answers are correct, all columns and rows will add to the same number.

A. NECKTIE        E. KATIE         I. LIGHTNING      M. SEVEN
B. SIX            F. BALLARD       J. SURVIVAL       N. BIRCH
C. RADIO          G. WOOD          K. JACKET         O. MANNERLY
D. MAP            H. BRIEFCASE     L. GRUBWORMS      P. RASPBERRIES

1. Erik ____; government survival instructor
2. Caused the problems on the trip
3. Bill____ said the government wanted Brian to teach them.
4. Showed the way to the trading post
5. Months after trip when Brian received Derek's gift
6. Months for Derek to recover
7. Contained the map, notebooks, and radio
8. Brian used it to make strips.
9. Left behind on trip down the river
10. First Food
11. Kind of gear left behind in the plane
12. ____ONE; radio station code name
13. Possible food
14. Brian said there could never be too much of it.
15. Name of the river
16. ____bark; used for food containers

| A= | B= | C= | D= |
| E= | F= | G= | H= |
| I= | J= | K= | L= |
| M= | N= | O= | P= |

The River Magic Squares 2 Answer Key

Match the definition with the vocabulary word. Put your answers in the magic squares below. When your answers are correct, all columns and rows will add to the same number.

A. NECKTIE
B. SIX
C. RADIO
D. MAP
E. KATIE
F. BALLARD
G. WOOD
H. BRIEFCASE
I. LIGHTNING
J. SURVIVAL
K. JACKET
L. GRUBWORMS
M. SEVEN
N. BIRCH
O. MANNERLY
P. RASPBERRIES

1. Erik ____; government survival instructor
2. Caused the problems on the trip
3. Bill ____ said the government wanted Brian to teach them.
4. Showed the way to the trading post
5. Months after trip when Brian received Derek's gift
6. Months for Derek to recover
7. Contained the map, notebooks, and radio
8. Brian used it to make strips.
9. Left behind on trip down the river
10. First Food
11. Kind of gear left behind in the plane
12. ____ONE; radio station code name
13. Possible food
14. Brian said there could never be too much of it.
15. Name of the river
16. ____bark; used for food containers

| A=15 | B=6  | C=9  | D=4  |
|------|------|------|------|
| E=12 | F=1  | G=14 | H=7  |
| I=2  | J=11 | K=8  | L=13 |
| M=5  | N=16 | O=3  | P=10 |

The River Magic Squares 3

Match the definition with the vocabulary word. Put your answers in the magic squares below. When your answers are correct, all columns and rows will add to the same number.

A. BRIAN
B. MANNERLY
C. JACKET
D. GRUBWORMS
E. LIGHTNING
F. RASPBERRIES
G. NECKTIE
H. MAP
I. SURVIVAL
J. KATIE
K. FOOD
L. HUNGER
M. CANOE
N. COUNSELOR
O. KNIVES
P. TENSION

1. Their only tools
2. Possible food
3. ____ONE; radio station code name
4. Caused the problems on the trip
5. Kind of gear left behind in the plane
6. First Food
7. The first part of the trip lacked it.
8. Brian used it to make strips.
9. Showed the way to the trading post
10. It was 'everything' in the wild, according to Brian.
11. Two-time wilderness survivor
12. Thought Brian was mentally injured
13. Bill____ said the government wanted Brian to teach them.
14. Gift to Brian from Derek
15. Name of the river
16. Brian's worst problem during The Time

| A= | B= | C= | D= |
| E= | F= | G= | H= |
| I= | J= | K= | L= |
| M= | N= | O= | P= |

The River Magic Squares 3 Answer Key

Match the definition with the vocabulary word. Put your answers in the magic squares below. When your answers are correct, all columns and rows will add to the same number.

A. BRIAN          E. LIGHTNING      I. SURVIVAL     M. CANOE
B. MANNERLY       F. RASPBERRIES    J. KATIE        N. COUNSELOR
C. JACKET         G. NECKTIE        K. FOOD         O. KNIVES
D. GRUBWORMS      H. MAP            L. HUNGER       P. TENSION

1. Their only tools
2. Possible food
3. ____ONE; radio station code name
4. Caused the problems on the trip
5. Kind of gear left behind in the plane
6. First Food
7. The first part of the trip lacked it.
8. Brian used it to make strips.
9. Showed the way to the trading post
10. It was 'everything' in the wild, according to Brian.
11. Two-time wilderness survivor
12. Thought Brian was mentally injured
13. Bill____ said the government wanted Brian to teach them.
14. Gift to Brian from Derek
15. Name of the river
16. Brian's worst problem during The Time

| A=11 | B=13 | C=8  | D=2  |
| ---- | ---- | ---- | ---- |
| E=4  | F=6  | G=15 | H=9  |
| I=5  | J=3  | K=10 | L=16 |
| M=14 | N=12 | O=1  | P=7  |

The River Magic Squares 4

Match the definition with the vocabulary word. Put your answers in the magic squares below. When your answers are correct, all columns and rows will add to the same number.

A. BOUGHS        E. CHUTE          I. TWO           M. NECKTIE
B. BALLARD       F. RASPBERRIES    J. TENSION       N. JACKET
C. COUNSELOR     G. COMA           K. FIRE          O. COOK
D. TWELVE        H. KATIE          L. CANOE         P. ROBESON

1. Pine ____; used for their beds
2. Brian used it to make strips.
3. The first part of the trip lacked it.
4. Dangerous, rocky water
5. Derek's medical state
6. Gift to Brian from Derek
7. Mr. ____ was about to get married.
8. Thought Brian was mentally injured
9. Brian's new hobby after first time in the wilderness
10. Pounds Brian lost
11. ____ONE; radio station code name
12. They didn't have one the first night.
13. Katie ____; Brian and Derek's code name
14. First Food
15. Erik ____; government survival instructor
16. Name of the river

| A= | B= | C= | D= |
| E= | F= | G= | H= |
| I= | J= | K= | L= |
| M= | N= | O= | P= |

The River Magic Squares 4 Answer Key

Match the definition with the vocabulary word. Put your answers in the magic squares below. When your answers are correct, all columns and rows will add to the same number.

A. BOUGHS
B. BALLARD
C. COUNSELOR
D. TWELVE
E. CHUTE
F. RASPBERRIES
G. COMA
H. KATIE
I. TWO
J. TENSION
K. FIRE
L. CANOE
M. NECKTIE
N. JACKET
O. COOK
P. ROBESON

1. Pine ____; used for their beds
2. Brian used it to make strips.
3. The first part of the trip lacked it.
4. Dangerous, rocky water
5. Derek's medical state
6. Gift to Brian from Derek
7. Mr. ____ was about to get married.
8. Thought Brian was mentally injured
9. Brian's new hobby after first time in the wilderness
10. Pounds Brian lost
11. ____ONE; radio station code name
12. They didn't have one the first night.
13. Katie ____; Brian and Derek's code name
14. First Food
15. Erik ____; government survival instructor
16. Name of the river

| | | | |
|---|---|---|---|
| A=1 | B=15 | C=8 | D=10 |
| E=4 | F=14 | G=5 | H=11 |
| I=13 | J=3 | K=12 | L=6 |
| M=16 | N=2 | O=9 | P=7 |

# The River Word Search 1

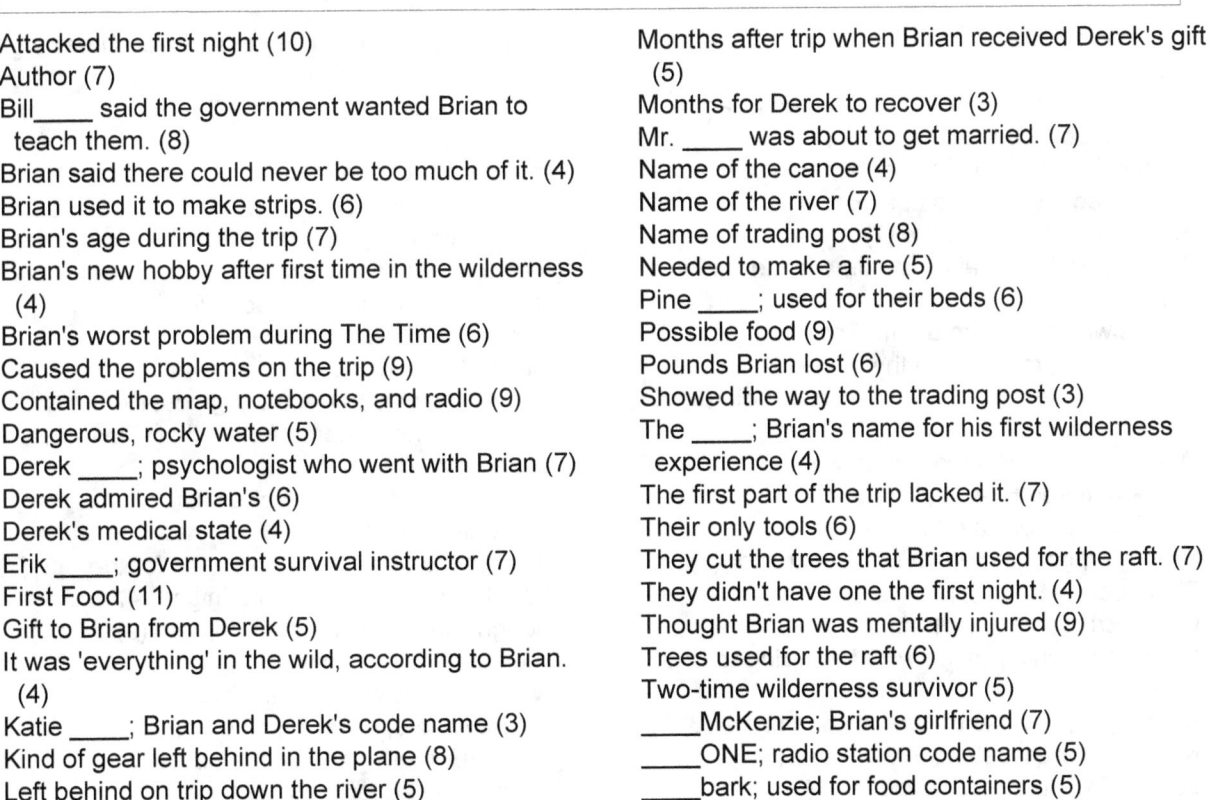

Attacked the first night (10)
Author (7)
Bill____ said the government wanted Brian to teach them. (8)
Brian said there could never be too much of it. (4)
Brian used it to make strips. (6)
Brian's age during the trip (7)
Brian's new hobby after first time in the wilderness (4)
Brian's worst problem during The Time (6)
Caused the problems on the trip (9)
Contained the map, notebooks, and radio (9)
Dangerous, rocky water (5)
Derek ____; psychologist who went with Brian (7)
Derek admired Brian's (6)
Derek's medical state (4)
Erik ____; government survival instructor (7)
First Food (11)
Gift to Brian from Derek (5)
It was 'everything' in the wild, according to Brian. (4)
Katie ____; Brian and Derek's code name (3)
Kind of gear left behind in the plane (8)
Left behind on trip down the river (5)

Months after trip when Brian received Derek's gift (5)
Months for Derek to recover (3)
Mr. ____ was about to get married. (7)
Name of the canoe (4)
Name of the river (7)
Name of trading post (8)
Needed to make a fire (5)
Pine ____; used for their beds (6)
Possible food (9)
Pounds Brian lost (6)
Showed the way to the trading post (3)
The ____; Brian's name for his first wilderness experience (4)
The first part of the trip lacked it. (7)
Their only tools (6)
They cut the trees that Brian used for the raft. (7)
They didn't have one the first night. (4)
Thought Brian was mentally injured (9)
Trees used for the raft (6)
Two-time wilderness survivor (5)
____McKenzie; Brian's girlfriend (7)
____ONE; radio station code name (5)
____bark; used for food containers (5)

# The River Word Search 1 Answer Key

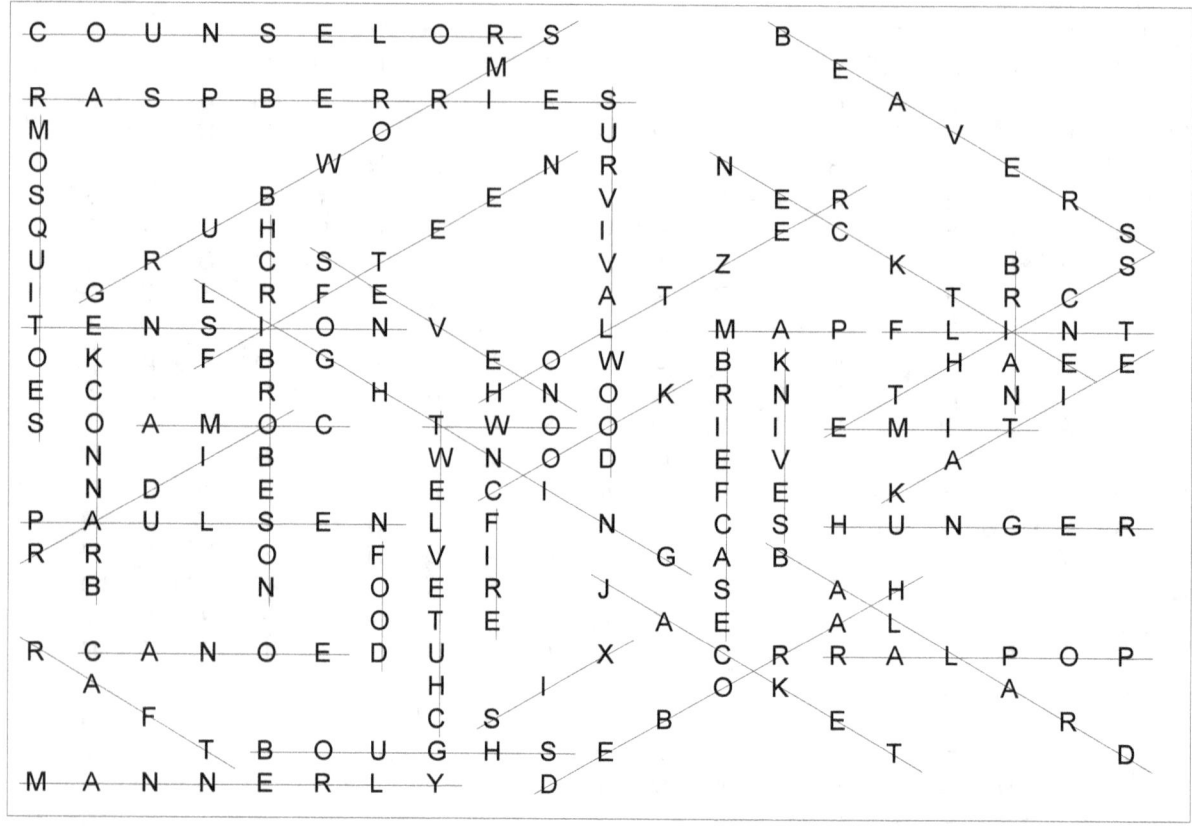

Attacked the first night (10)
Author (7)
Bill____ said the government wanted Brian to teach them. (8)
Brian said there could never be too much of it. (4)
Brian used it to make strips. (6)
Brian's age during the trip (7)
Brian's new hobby after first time in the wilderness (4)
Brian's worst problem during The Time (6)
Caused the problems on the trip (9)
Contained the map, notebooks, and radio (9)
Dangerous, rocky water (5)
Derek ____; psychologist who went with Brian (7)
Derek admired Brian's (6)
Derek's medical state (4)
Erik ____; government survival instructor (7)
First Food (11)
Gift to Brian from Derek (5)
It was 'everything' in the wild, according to Brian. (4)
Katie ____; Brian and Derek's code name (3)
Kind of gear left behind in the plane (8)
Left behind on trip down the river (5)

Months after trip when Brian received Derek's gift (5)
Months for Derek to recover (3)
Mr. ____ was about to get married. (7)
Name of the canoe (4)
Name of the river (7)
Name of trading post (8)
Needed to make a fire (5)
Pine ____; used for their beds (6)
Possible food (9)
Pounds Brian lost (6)
Showed the way to the trading post (3)
The ____; Brian's name for his first wilderness experience (4)
The first part of the trip lacked it. (7)
Their only tools (6)
They cut the trees that Brian used for the raft. (7)
They didn't have one the first night. (4)
Thought Brian was mentally injured (9)
Trees used for the raft (6)
Two-time wilderness survivor (5)
____McKenzie; Brian's girlfriend (7)
____ONE; radio station code name (5)
____bark; used for food containers (5)

30
Copyrighted

# The River Word Search 2

```
B A L L A R D F B J W G B R K N I V E S
G C M M Y D K I Z R H N N T O V R N W J
S H W D Q F D F V B I F J K G B F N F Z
B S R S K N Q T P R N E Y C S Y E N J C
N L M L B D T E R V B S F D N X T S G T
L B A Z R L B E M Y P P G C X N H P O Z
L T N J A T P N Y L V Z M B A E X K V N
E K N G N T F F E M R N E V E S R A F T
I K E W N S J I W A W D V L U L E T G F
T X R O O H T H D L G F C R F U M E R N
K Y L O C A W I Y Y S L V E I A J N U W
C R Y D K B O U G H S I D G R P V S B S
E O A W L N R N M E V N X N E M C I W C
N M O S Q F I N O A G T F U C I R O O B
T A D K P N Y T L C O M A H H C R N R D
H P T J T B I Q P Y G Q U T H A A I M L
B V F H K U E S J V T T E G L T A N S H
L E G R Q H A R O B E D K P J N F O O D
T I A S Y S C W R C X B O C A K D L D E
L I O V T Y Q S Y I G P S Q C W T N M Y
X M M R E V L E W T E R G G K Z X W D G
X F P E X R B Q P S H S R P E F N Y G G
T J T R X D S G J J M P Z R T D W F V F
C G T P Z H F X R C O U N S E L O R Q H
```

Attacked the first night (10)
Author (7)
Bill____ said the government wanted Brian to teach them. (8)
Brian said there could never be too much of it. (4)
Brian used it to make strips. (6)
Brian's age during the trip (7)
Brian's new hobby after first time in the wilderness (4)
Brian's worst problem during The Time (6)
Caused the problems on the trip (9)
Contained the map, notebooks, and radio (9)
Dangerous, rocky water (5)
Derek ____; psychologist who went with Brian (7)
Derek admired Brian's (6)
Derek's medical state (4)
Erik ____; government survival instructor (7)
First Food (11)
Gift to Brian from Derek (5)
It was 'everything' in the wild, according to Brian. (4)
Katie ____; Brian and Derek's code name (3)
Kind of gear left behind in the plane (8)
Left behind on trip down the river (5)
Months after trip when Brian received Derek's gift (5)
Months for Derek to recover (3)
Mr. ____ was about to get married. (7)
Name of the canoe (4)
Name of the river (7)
Name of trading post (8)
Needed to make a fire (5)
Pine ____; used for their beds (6)
Possible food (9)
Pounds Brian lost (6)
Showed the way to the trading post (3)
The ____; Brian's name for his first wilderness experience (4)
The first part of the trip lacked it. (7)
Their only tools (6)
They cut the trees that Brian used for the raft. (7)
They didn't have one the first night. (4)
Thought Brian was mentally injured (9)
Trees used for the raft (6)
Two-time wilderness survivor (5)
____McKenzie; Brian's girlfriend (7)
____ONE; radio station code name (5)
____bark; used for food containers (5)

# The River Word Search 2 Answer Key

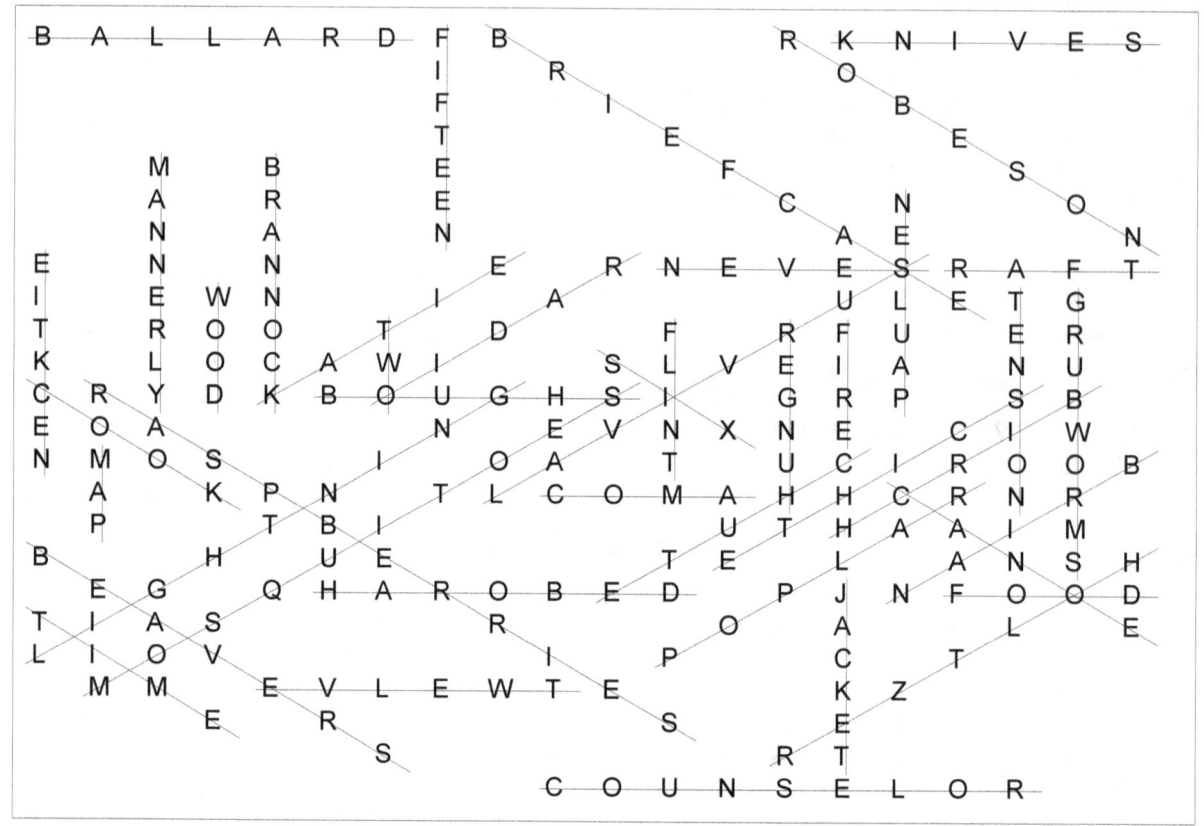

Attacked the first night (10)
Author (7)
Bill____ said the government wanted Brian to teach them. (8)
Brian said there could never be too much of it. (4)
Brian used it to make strips. (6)
Brian's age during the trip (7)
Brian's new hobby after first time in the wilderness (4)
Brian's worst problem during The Time (6)
Caused the problems on the trip (9)
Contained the map, notebooks, and radio (9)
Dangerous, rocky water (5)
Derek ____; psychologist who went with Brian (7)
Derek admired Brian's (6)
Derek's medical state (4)
Erik ____; government survival instructor (7)
First Food (11)
Gift to Brian from Derek (5)
It was 'everything' in the wild, according to Brian. (4)
Katie ____; Brian and Derek's code name (3)
Kind of gear left behind in the plane (8)
Left behind on trip down the river (5)

Months after trip when Brian received Derek's gift (5)
Months for Derek to recover (3)
Mr. ____ was about to get married. (7)
Name of the canoe (4)
Name of the river (7)
Name of trading post (8)
Needed to make a fire (5)
Pine ____; used for their beds (6)
Possible food (9)
Pounds Brian lost (6)
Showed the way to the trading post (3)
The ____; Brian's name for his first wilderness experience (4)
The first part of the trip lacked it. (7)
Their only tools (6)
They cut the trees that Brian used for the raft. (7)
They didn't have one the first night. (4)
Thought Brian was mentally injured (9)
Trees used for the raft (6)
Two-time wilderness survivor (5)
____McKenzie; Brian's girlfriend (7)
____ONE; radio station code name (5)
____bark; used for food containers (5)

## The River Word Search 3

```
M B R I E F C A S E D K J M P Y J H C C
G R W J Z D I Q T N F M Y P P G K C R Z
N X Y X G W D F S M M L D R N C A T N S
G S Y X M E D D T T R N W A N S T L R C
R A S P B E R R I E S F I E E R I F V M
X D N O E G V P N N E R L M K G E X T K
P B R Y A N T N F S B N D I H D G W J H
D A H Z V W A W O I N H T T N E V E S C
H H U B E M V S O O Y E N V P T N P S G
K H F L R Q T M D N K I R F X U F N M P
N R V C S N T C P C N E B Z C H Z H X M
I E C O C E E G A G G H Y O M C C Z J F
V Z W O K O N J C N D R M T U R F Q K D
E T F K N T F R U F K A U R I G W J S Y
S L F A W W L H A B N M R B O N H K V C
V O C M Z O C T D D N B A M W B C S P Y
M H F J L J O F T L I L F A D O E N V M
D H Q P S J U D M M L O T P N X R S X G
V Z G K M Y N S D A G N R N E N L M O M
E T H I C S S U R V I V A L C P G W S N
S W G W S X E D C L X R L Q K N N M N L
B M C G F D L N T T B F P K T V D K D Z
H Z Z T S E O T I U Q S O M I R Y C X Q
W K X P P L R W D G L P P B E G P S K Q
```

| | | | | |
|---|---|---|---|---|
| BALLARD | COMA | GRUBWORMS | MOSQUITOES | SIX |
| BEAVERS | COOK | HOLTZER | NECKTIE | SURVIVAL |
| BIRCH | COUNSELOR | HUNGER | PAULSEN | TENSION |
| BOUGHS | DEBORAH | JACKET | POPLAR | TIME |
| BRANNOCK | ETHICS | KATIE | RADIO | TWELVE |
| BRIAN | FIFTEEN | KNIVES | RAFT | TWO |
| BRIEFCASE | FIRE | LIGHTNING | RASPBERRIES | WOOD |
| CANOE | FLINT | MANNERLY | ROBESON | |
| CHUTE | FOOD | MAP | SEVEN | |

The River Word Search 3 Answer Key

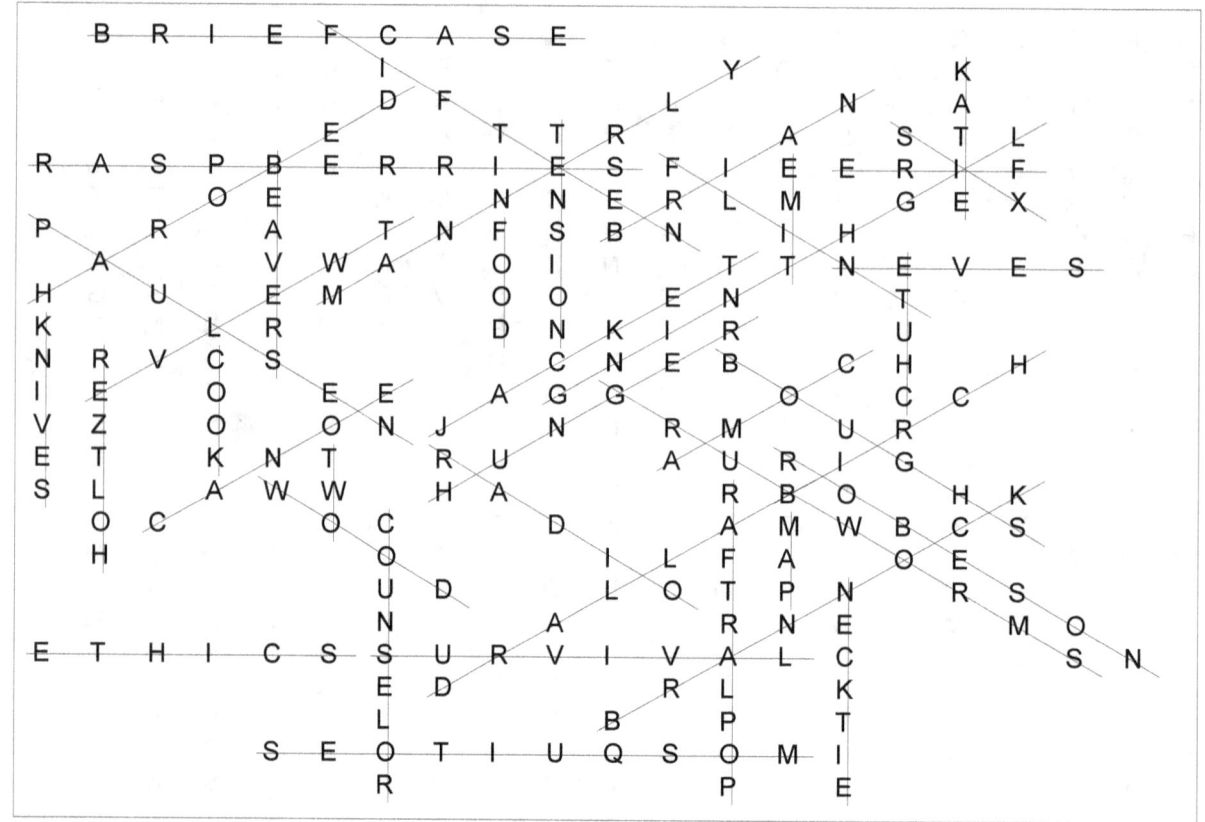

| BALLARD | COMA | GRUBWORMS | MOSQUITOES | SIX |
| BEAVERS | COOK | HOLTZER | NECKTIE | SURVIVAL |
| BIRCH | COUNSELOR | HUNGER | PAULSEN | TENSION |
| BOUGHS | DEBORAH | JACKET | POPLAR | TIME |
| BRANNOCK | ETHICS | KATIE | RADIO | TWELVE |
| BRIAN | FIFTEEN | KNIVES | RAFT | TWO |
| BRIEFCASE | FIRE | LIGHTNING | RASPBERRIES | WOOD |
| CANOE | FLINT | MANNERLY | ROBESON | |
| CHUTE | FOOD | MAP | SEVEN | |

## The River Word Search 4

```
C M X R E Z T L O H S R E V A E B W B Z
F O Q B T S J Z R K Z V P Z C H Q O A J
J F M R H E Q T X C L R F S Q C Q O L Y
J L D A I O F M R E R A J P R E G D L Z
Y I Z N C T K W W V A F B P R S Q K A M
T N Q E S I W T D H S T K I T I K C R S
F T L S K U Y O K J P Y F P R X V O D Q
P X Z L P Q V S Y C B G B P N C J N J T
F C O U N S E L O R E R K K E S H N Q P
F Q F A X O S M C F R U X M C U Y A S D
L Y I P Y M T Q F P R B D H K R N R R Q
Q Z F K P T S R J H I W N F T V P B X M
R L T N D E K C O B E O P W I I M R M K
Y I E B V D A V Y B S R M V E V P I B S
D G E E J D T N C B E M X A M A B A G N
J H N M B R I E F C A S E D P L G N Y W
R T G T A D E S L N M P O C B G O Z G X
P N I D Z N J K J P N O L N K I H Z V T
D I X M L R N T S F F P Q H S W R P P S
K N I V E S R E G N U H L N C O O K H Q
V G G O T R A K R Y L C E Q Q P L G X H
H W N X U P D C T L G T H G L R U Y D M
J A S C H V I A X C Y S H A R O B E D P
C S M X C K O J R C F B R N B Y N X J B
```

| | | | | |
|---|---|---|---|---|
| BALLARD | COMA | GRUBWORMS | MOSQUITOES | SIX |
| BEAVERS | COOK | HOLTZER | NECKTIE | SURVIVAL |
| BIRCH | COUNSELOR | HUNGER | PAULSEN | TENSION |
| BOUGHS | DEBORAH | JACKET | POPLAR | TIME |
| BRANNOCK | ETHICS | KATIE | RADIO | TWELVE |
| BRIAN | FIFTEEN | KNIVES | RAFT | TWO |
| BRIEFCASE | FIRE | LIGHTNING | RASPBERRIES | WOOD |
| CANOE | FLINT | MANNERLY | ROBESON | |
| CHUTE | FOOD | MAP | SEVEN | |

The River Word Search 4 Answer Key

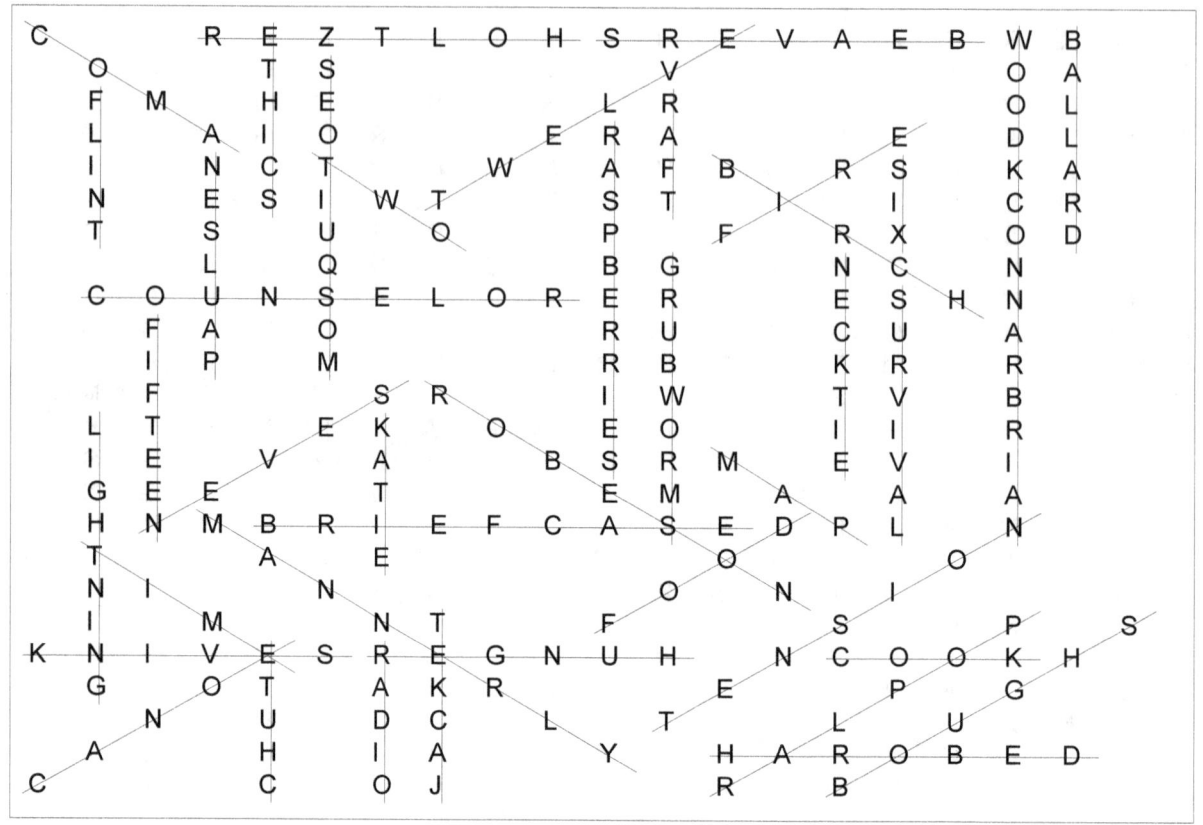

| BALLARD | COMA | GRUBWORMS | MOSQUITOES | SIX |
| BEAVERS | COOK | HOLTZER | NECKTIE | SURVIVAL |
| BIRCH | COUNSELOR | HUNGER | PAULSEN | TENSION |
| BOUGHS | DEBORAH | JACKET | POPLAR | TIME |
| BRANNOCK | ETHICS | KATIE | RADIO | TWELVE |
| BRIAN | FIFTEEN | KNIVES | RAFT | TWO |
| BRIEFCASE | FIRE | LIGHTNING | RASPBERRIES | WOOD |
| CANOE | FLINT | MANNERLY | ROBESON | |
| CHUTE | FOOD | MAP | SEVEN | |

The River Crossword 1

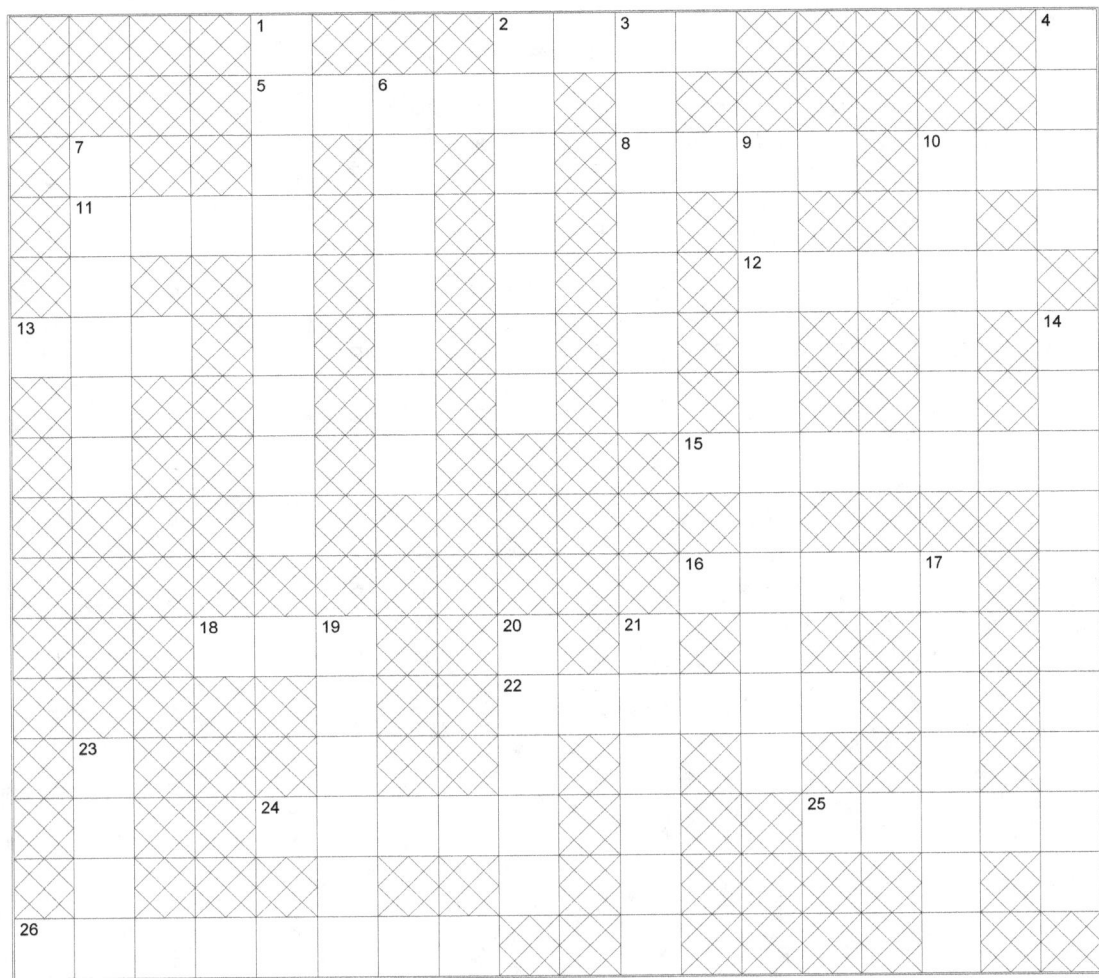

Across
2. Name of the canoe
5. Left behind on trip down the river
8. They didn't have one the first night.
10. Katie ____; Brian and Derek's code name
11. The ____; Brian's name for his first wilderness experience
12. Months after trip when Brian received Derek's gift
13. Months for Derek to recover
15. They cut the trees that Brian used for the raft.
16. Two-time wilderness survivor
18. Showed the way to the trading post
22. Brian's worst problem during The Time
24. Needed to make a fire
25. ____ONE; radio station code name
26. Bill____ said the government wanted Brian to teach them.

Down
1. Contained the map, notebooks, and radio
2. Mr. ____ was about to get married.
3. Brian's age during the trip
4. Brian's new hobby after first time in the wilderness
6. ____McKenzie; Brian's girlfriend
7. Derek admired Brian's
9. First Food
10. Pounds Brian lost
14. Attacked the first night
17. Name of the river
19. Trees used for the raft
20. Dangerous, rocky water
21. Their only tools
23. Derek's medical state

## The River Crossword 1 Answer Key

|   |   |   | 1 B |   |   | 2 R | A | 3 F | T |   |   |   | 4 C |
|---|---|---|---|---|---|---|---|---|---|---|---|---|---|
|   |   | 5 R | A | 6 D | I | O |   | I |   |   |   |   | O |
|   | 7 E |   | I |   | E | B |   | 8 F | 9 I | R | E | 10 T | W | O |
|   | 11 T | I | M | E |   | B |   | E |   | T |   | A |   | W |   | K |
|   | H |   |   |   | F |   | O |   | S |   | E |   | 12 S | E | V | E | N |
| 13 S | I | X |   | C |   | A |   | R |   | O |   | E |   | P |   | L |   | 14 M |
|   | C |   |   |   | A |   | A |   | N |   | N |   | B |   | V |   | O |
|   | S |   |   |   | S |   | H |   |   |   |   | 15 B | E | A | V | E | R | S |
|   |   |   |   |   | E |   |   |   |   |   |   | R |   |   |   |   |   | Q |
|   |   |   |   |   |   |   |   |   |   | 16 B | R | I | A | 17 N |   | U |
|   |   |   | 18 M | A | 19 P |   | 20 C |   | 21 K |   | I |   | E |   | I |
|   |   |   |   |   | O |   | 22 H | U | N | G | E | R |   | C |   | T |
|   |   | 23 C |   |   | P |   | U |   | I |   | S |   | K |   | O |
|   |   | O |   | 24 F | L | I | N | T |   | V |   |   | 25 K | A | T | I | E |
|   |   | M |   |   | A |   |   |   | E |   |   |   |   |   | I |   | S |
| 26 M | A | N | N | E | R | L | Y |   | S |   |   |   | E |

**Across**
- 2. Name of the canoe
- 5. Left behind on trip down the river
- 8. They didn't have one the first night.
- 10. Katie ____; Brian and Derek's code name
- 11. The ____; Brian's name for his first wilderness experience
- 12. Months after trip when Brian received Derek's gift
- 13. Months for Derek to recover
- 15. They cut the trees that Brian used for the raft.
- 16. Two-time wilderness survivor
- 18. Showed the way to the trading post
- 22. Brian's worst problem during The Time
- 24. Needed to make a fire
- 25. ____ONE; radio station code name
- 26. Bill____ said the government wanted Brian to teach them.

**Down**
- 1. Contained the map, notebooks, and radio
- 2. Mr. ____ was about to get married.
- 3. Brian's age during the trip
- 4. Brian's new hobby after first time in the wilderness
- 6. ____McKenzie; Brian's girlfriend
- 7. Derek admired Brian's
- 9. First Food
- 10. Pounds Brian lost
- 14. Attacked the first night
- 17. Name of the river
- 19. Trees used for the raft
- 20. Dangerous, rocky water
- 21. Their only tools
- 23. Derek's medical state

Copyrighted

The River Crossword 2

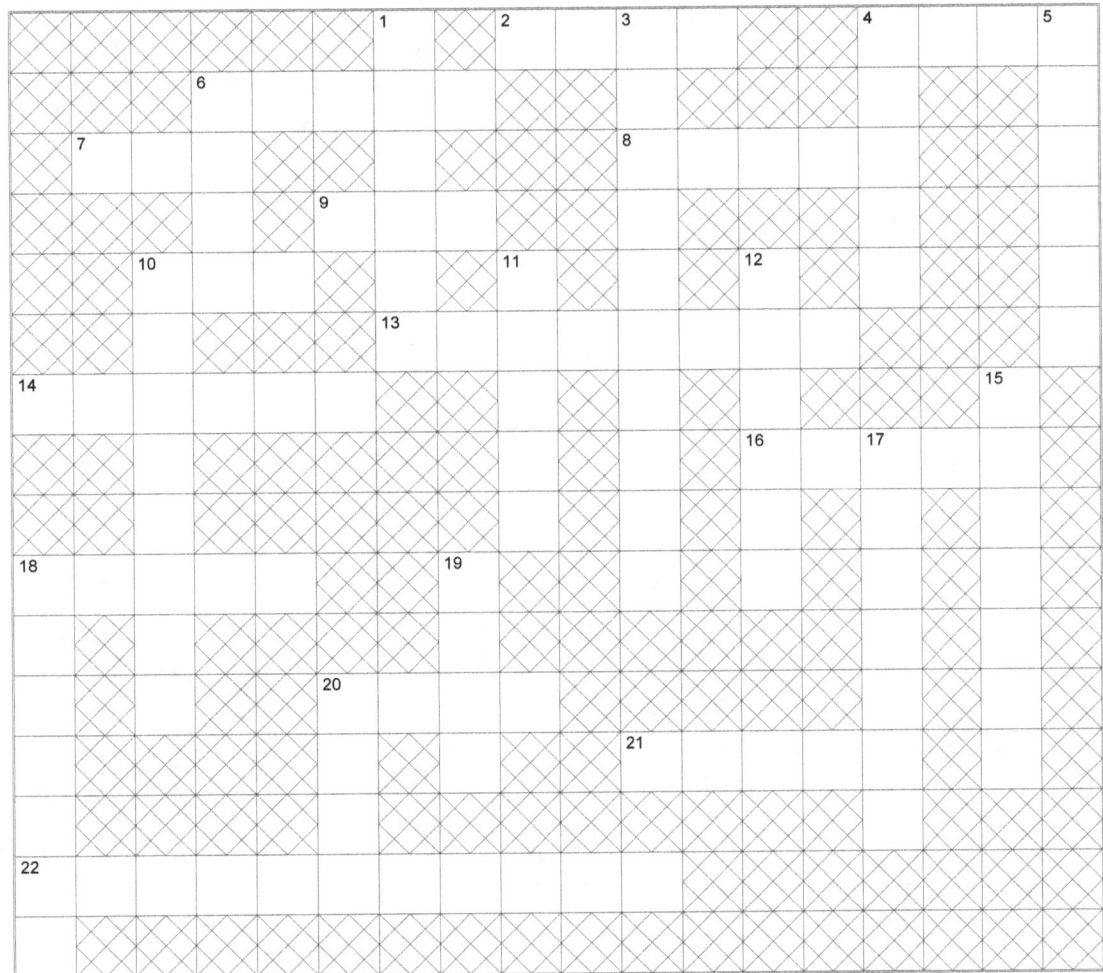

Across
2. The ____; Brian's name for his first wilderness experience
4. Brian's new hobby after first time in the wilderness
6. Dangerous, rocky water
7. Katie ____; Brian and Derek's code name
8. Months after trip when Brian received Derek's gift
9. Months for Derek to recover
10. Showed the way to the trading post
13. Kind of gear left behind in the plane
14. Brian's worst problem during The Time
16. ____ONE; radio station code name
18. ____bark; used for food containers
20. It was 'everything' in the wild, according to Brian.
21. Left behind on trip down the river
22. First Food

Down
1. Derek admired Brian's
3. Attacked the first night
4. Gift to Brian from Derek
5. Their only tools
6. Derek's medical state
10. Bill____ said the government wanted Brian to teach them.
11. Two-time wilderness survivor
12. Brian used it to make strips.
15. Name of the river
17. The first part of the trip lacked it.
18. Erik ____; government survival instructor
19. Brian said there could never be too much of it.
20. They didn't have one the first night.

# The River Crossword 2 Answer Key

|    |    |    |    |    |    | 1 E | 2 T | I  | 3 M | E  |    | 4 C | O  | O  | 5 K |
|----|----|----|----|----|----|-----|-----|----|-----|----|----|-----|----|----|-----|
|    |    |    | 6 C | H  | U  | T   | E   |    | O   |    |    | A   |    |    | N   |
|    | 7 T | W  | O  |    |    | H   |     |    | 8 S | E  | V  | E   | N  |    | I   |
|    |    |    | M  |    | 9 S | I   | X   |    | Q   |    |    | O   |    |    | V   |
|    |    | 10 M | A  | P  |    | C   |     | 11 B |    | 12 J |    | E   |    |    | E   |
|    |    | A  |    |    |    | 13 S | U   | R  | V   | I  | V  | A   | L  |    | S   |
| 14 H | U  | N  | G  | E  | R  |     |     | I  |     | T  |    | C   |    | 15 N |     |
|    |    | N  |    |    |    |     |     | A  |     | O  |    | 16 K | A  | T  | 17 I | E |
|    |    | E  |    |    |    |     |     | N  |     | E  |    | E   |    | E  |     |
| 18 B | I  | R  | C  | H  |    | 19 W |     |    |     | S  |    | T   |    | N  | K   |
| A  |    | L  |    |    |    | O   |     |    |     |    |    |     |    | S  | T   |
| L  |    | Y  |    | 20 F | O  | O   | D   |    |     |    |    |     |    | I  | I   |
| L  |    |    |    | I   |    | D   |     |    |     | 21 R | A  | D   | I  | O  |    | E |
| A  |    |    |    | R   |    |     |     |    |     |    |    |     |    | N  |     |
| 22 R | A  | S  | P  | B   | E  | R   | R   | I  | E   | S  |    |     |    |    |     |
| D  |    |    |    |     |    |     |     |    |     |    |    |     |    |    |     |

**Across**
2. The ____; Brian's name for his first wilderness experience
4. Brian's new hobby after first time in the wilderness
6. Dangerous, rocky water
7. Katie ____; Brian and Derek's code name
8. Months after trip when Brian received Derek's gift
9. Months for Derek to recover
10. Showed the way to the trading post
13. Kind of gear left behind in the plane
14. Brian's worst problem during The Time
16. ____ONE; radio station code name
18. ____bark; used for food containers
20. It was 'everything' in the wild, according to Brian.
21. Left behind on trip down the river
22. First Food

**Down**
1. Derek admired Brian's
3. Attacked the first night
4. Gift to Brian from Derek
5. Their only tools
6. Derek's medical state
10. Bill____ said the government wanted Brian to teach them.
11. Two-time wilderness survivor
12. Brian used it to make strips.
15. Name of the river
17. The first part of the trip lacked it.
18. Erik ____; government survival instructor
19. Brian said there could never be too much of it.
20. They didn't have one the first night.

# The River Crossword 3

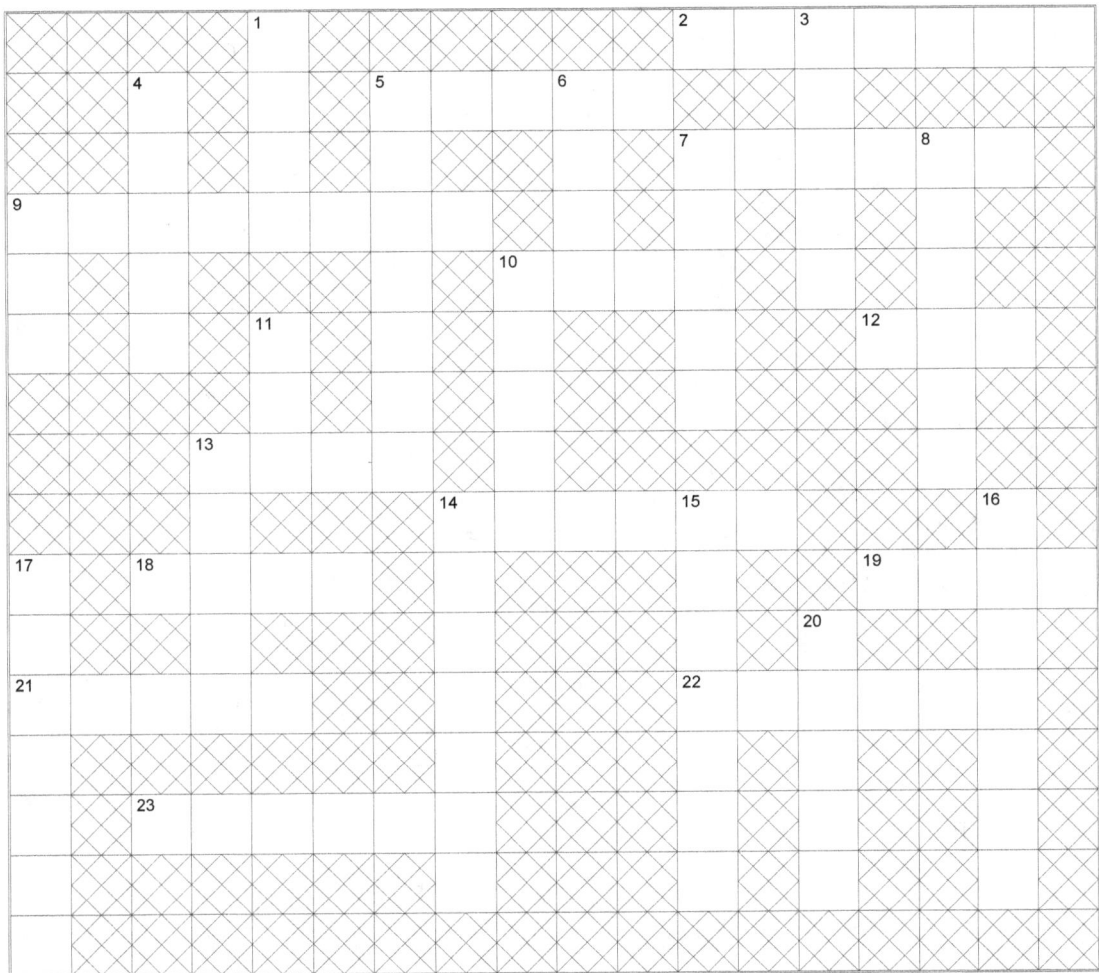

## Across
2. ____McKenzie; Brian's girlfriend
5. ____bark; used for food containers
7. Their only tools
9. Bill____ said the government wanted Brian to teach them.
10. Name of the canoe
12. Months for Derek to recover
13. It was 'everything' in the wild, according to Brian.
14. Pine ____; used for their beds
18. The ____; Brian's name for his first wilderness experience
19. Brian's new hobby after first time in the wilderness
21. Dangerous, rocky water
22. Pounds Brian lost
23. Trees used for the raft

## Down
1. They didn't have one the first night.
3. Two-time wilderness survivor
4. Gift to Brian from Derek
5. Erik ____; government survival instructor
6. Derek's medical state
7. ____ONE; radio station code name
8. Derek admired Brian's
9. Showed the way to the trading post
10. Left behind on trip down the river
11. Katie ____; Brian and Derek's code name
13. Needed to make a fire
14. They cut the trees that Brian used for the raft.
15. Derek ____; psychologist who went with Brian
16. Mr. ____ was about to get married.
17. Name of the river
20. Months after trip when Brian received Derek's gift

The River Crossword 3 Answer Key

|   |   |   | 1 F |   | 5 B | I | 6 C | H | 2 D | E | 3 B | O | R | A | H |
|---|---|---|---|---|---|---|---|---|---|---|---|---|---|---|---|
|   |   | 4 C | I |   |   |   |   |   | 7 K | N | I | V | 8 E | S |   |
| 9 M | A | N | N | E | R | L | Y |   | A | | A |   | T | | |
| A | | O | | | | 10 R | A | F | T | | N | | H | | |
| P | | E | 11 T | A | | A | | | I | | | 12 S | I | X | |
| | | | W | | R | D | | | E | | | C | | | |
| | 13 F | O | O | D | | I | | | | | | S | | | |
| | | | L | | | 14 B | O | 15 H | G | H | S | | 16 R | | |
| 17 N | 18 T | I | M | E | | E | | O | | | | 19 C | O | O | K |
| E | | N | | | | A | | L | | 20 S | | | B | | |
| 21 C | H | U | T | E | | V | | | | 22 T | W | E | L | V | E |
| K | | | | | | E | | | | Z | | V | | S | |
| T | 23 P | O | P | L | A | R | | | | E | | E | | O | |
| I | | | | | | S | | | | R | | N | | N | |
| E | | | | | | | | | | | | | | | |

Across
2. ____McKenzie; Brian's girlfriend
5. ____bark; used for food containers
7. Their only tools
9. Bill____ said the government wanted Brian to teach them.
10. Name of the canoe
12. Months for Derek to recover
13. It was 'everything' in the wild, according to Brian.
14. Pine ____; used for their beds
18. The ____; Brian's name for his first wilderness experience
19. Brian's new hobby after first time in the wilderness
21. Dangerous, rocky water
22. Pounds Brian lost
23. Trees used for the raft

Down
1. They didn't have one the first night.
3. Two-time wilderness survivor
4. Gift to Brian from Derek
5. Erik ____; government survival instructor
6. Derek's medical state
7. ____ONE; radio station code name
8. Derek admired Brian's
9. Showed the way to the trading post
10. Left behind on trip down the river
11. Katie ____; Brian and Derek's code name
13. Needed to make a fire
14. They cut the trees that Brian used for the raft.
15. Derek ____; psychologist who went with Brian
16. Mr. ____ was about to get married.
17. Name of the river
20. Months after trip when Brian received Derek's gift

The River Crossword 4

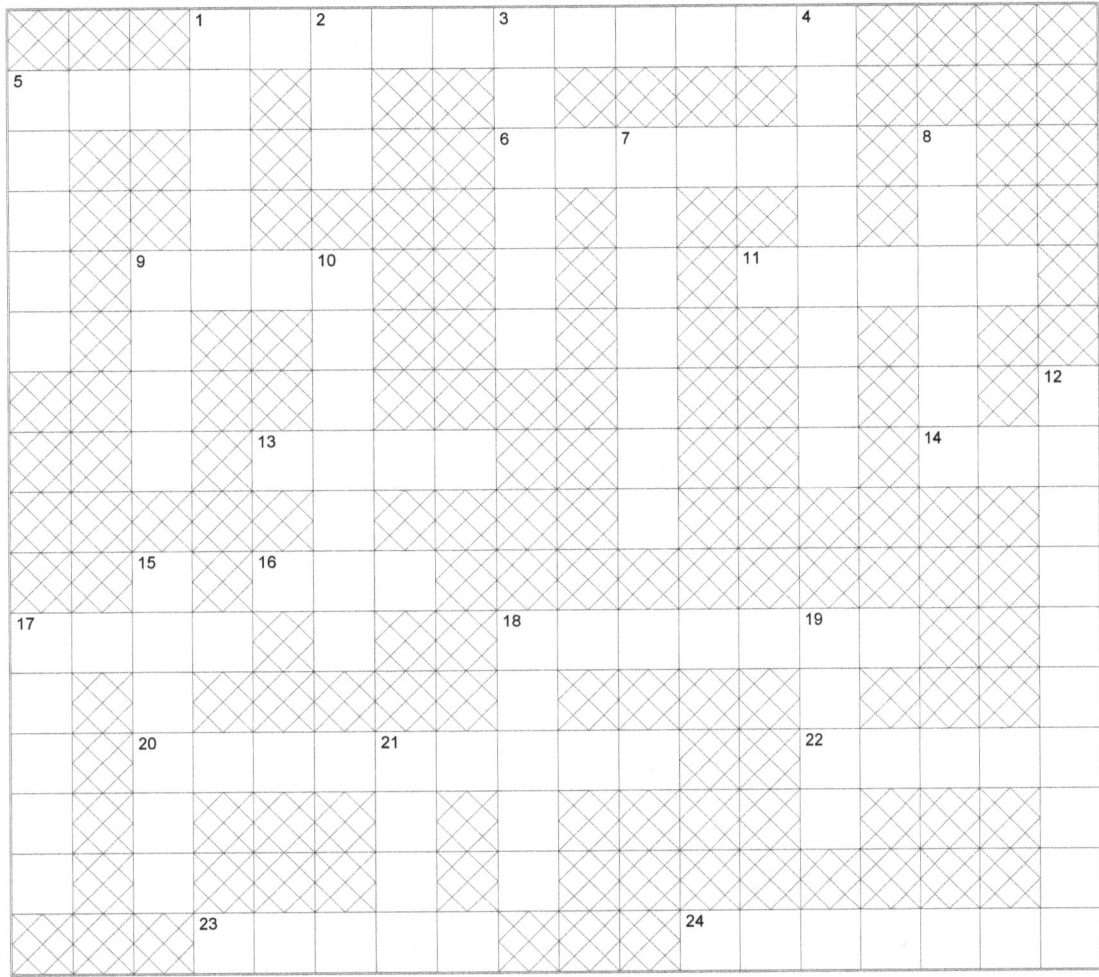

Across
1. First Food
5. Derek's medical state
6. Brian's worst problem during The Time
9. It was 'everything' in the wild, according to Brian.
11. ____bark; used for food containers
13. Brian said there could never be too much of it.
14. Katie ____; Brian and Derek's code name
16. Showed the way to the trading post
17. Brian's new hobby after first time in the wilderness
18. Erik ____; government survival instructor
20. Caused the problems on the trip
22. Needed to make a fire
23. Months after trip when Brian received Derek's gift
24. They cut the trees that Brian used for the raft.

Down
1. Left behind on trip down the river
2. Months for Derek to recover
3. Derek admired Brian's
4. Kind of gear left behind in the plane
5. Gift to Brian from Derek
7. Name of the river
8. Brian used it to make strips.
9. They didn't have one the first night.
10. ____McKenzie; Brian's girlfriend
12. Attacked the first night
15. Trees used for the raft
17. Dangerous, rocky water
18. Two-time wilderness survivor
19. Name of the canoe
21. The ____; Brian's name for his first wilderness experience

The River Crossword 4 Answer Key

|   |   |   | 1 R | 2 S | P | B | 3 E | R | R | I | E | 4 S |   |   |
|---|---|---|---|---|---|---|---|---|---|---|---|---|---|---|
| 5 C | O | M | A |   | I |   | T |   |   |   |   | U |   |   |
| A |   |   | D | X |   | 6 H | 7 U | N | G | E | R | 8 J |   |   |
| N |   |   | I |   |   | I | E |   |   |   | V | A |   |   |
| O |   | 9 F | O | 10 O | D |   | C |   | 11 B | I | R | C | H |   |
| E |   | I |   | E |   | C | K |   | V |   |   | K |   | 12 M |
|   |   | R |   | B |   | S | T |   | A |   | 14 E | E | W | O |
|   |   | E | 13 W | O | O | D |   | I |   | L | T | W | O | S |
|   |   |   |   | R |   |   |   | E |   |   |   |   |   | Q |
|   |   | 15 P | 16 M | A | P |   |   |   |   |   |   |   |   |   |
| 17 C | O | O | K |   | H |   | 18 B | A | L | L | 19 A | R | D | U |
| H |   | P |   |   |   | R |   |   |   | A |   |   | I |   |
| U | 20 L | I | G | H | T | 21 T | N | I | N | G | 22 F | L | I | N | T |
| T | A |   |   | I |   | A |   |   |   | T |   |   | O |   |
| E | R |   |   | M |   | N |   |   |   |   |   |   | E |   |
|   |   | 23 S | E | V | E | N |   | 24 B | E | A | V | E | R | S |

Across
1. First Food
5. Derek's medical state
6. Brian's worst problem during The Time
9. It was 'everything' in the wild, according to Brian.
11. ____bark; used for food containers
13. Brian said there could never be too much of it.
14. Katie ____; Brian and Derek's code name
16. Showed the way to the trading post
17. Brian's new hobby after first time in the wilderness
18. Erik ____; government survival instructor
20. Caused the problems on the trip
22. Needed to make a fire
23. Months after trip when Brian received Derek's gift
24. They cut the trees that Brian used for the raft.

Down
1. Left behind on trip down the river
2. Months for Derek to recover
3. Derek admired Brian's
4. Kind of gear left behind in the plane
5. Gift to Brian from Derek
7. Name of the river
8. Brian used it to make strips.
9. They didn't have one the first night.
10. ____McKenzie; Brian's girlfriend
12. Attacked the first night
15. Trees used for the raft
17. Dangerous, rocky water
18. Two-time wilderness survivor
19. Name of the canoe
21. The ____; Brian's name for his first wilderness experience

The River

| SEVEN | SURVIVAL | WOOD | GRUBWORMS | MOSQUITOES |
|---|---|---|---|---|
| PAULSEN | CHUTE | BRIEFCASE | BEAVERS | JACKET |
| BIRCH | FIFTEEN | FREE SPACE | SIX | POPLAR |
| NECKTIE | MANNERLY | FOOD | TENSION | HOLTZER |
| FLINT | DEBORAH | RASPBERRIES | COOK | MAP |

The River

| KNIVES | RADIO | BRIAN | FIRE | TWELVE |
|---|---|---|---|---|
| HUNGER | ETHICS | RAFT | BRANNOCK | LIGHTNING |
| COMA | CANOE | FREE SPACE | KATIE | COUNSELOR |
| TWO | ROBESON | TIME | MAP | COOK |
| RASPBERRIES | DEBORAH | FLINT | HOLTZER | TENSION |

## The River

| CHUTE | MOSQUITOES | LIGHTNING | FIRE | BOUGHS |
|---|---|---|---|---|
| COMA | BEAVERS | FIFTEEN | RADIO | TIME |
| WOOD | ROBESON | FREE SPACE | HOLTZER | COUNSELOR |
| JACKET | SEVEN | KNIVES | BALLARD | SIX |
| KATIE | NECKTIE | TWELVE | HUNGER | MANNERLY |

## The River

| GRUBWORMS | ETHICS | RASPBERRIES | PAULSEN | COOK |
|---|---|---|---|---|
| BRANNOCK | FOOD | CANOE | POPLAR | SURVIVAL |
| FLINT | MAP | FREE SPACE | BRIAN | DEBORAH |
| TWO | TENSION | BRIEFCASE | MANNERLY | HUNGER |
| TWELVE | NECKTIE | KATIE | SIX | BALLARD |

The River

| JACKET | POPLAR | TWO | BIRCH | SIX |
|---|---|---|---|---|
| TWELVE | COMA | MOSQUITOES | HUNGER | PAULSEN |
| NECKTIE | RAFT | FREE SPACE | BOUGHS | FOOD |
| HOLTZER | KNIVES | MAP | LIGHTNING | ROBESON |
| KATIE | GRUBWORMS | TENSION | COOK | WOOD |

The River

| TIME | DEBORAH | COUNSELOR | CHUTE | FLINT |
|---|---|---|---|---|
| RASPBERRIES | MANNERLY | FIRE | SURVIVAL | CANOE |
| BRIAN | SEVEN | FREE SPACE | ETHICS | BEAVERS |
| BALLARD | FIFTEEN | BRANNOCK | WOOD | COOK |
| TENSION | GRUBWORMS | KATIE | ROBESON | LIGHTNING |

The River

| COMA | FOOD | TWELVE | ETHICS | RAFT |
| --- | --- | --- | --- | --- |
| CHUTE | RASPBERRIES | HUNGER | LIGHTNING | FIRE |
| SURVIVAL | BRIEFCASE | FREE SPACE | JACKET | NECKTIE |
| GRUBWORMS | TWO | BRANNOCK | SIX | KATIE |
| POPLAR | CANOE | TENSION | MANNERLY | BOUGHS |

The River

| COOK | BRIAN | MOSQUITOES | WOOD | HOLTZER |
| --- | --- | --- | --- | --- |
| COUNSELOR | FIFTEEN | SEVEN | MAP | BIRCH |
| DEBORAH | FLINT | FREE SPACE | TIME | KNIVES |
| BALLARD | PAULSEN | ROBESON | BOUGHS | MANNERLY |
| TENSION | CANOE | POPLAR | KATIE | SIX |

The River

| BRIAN | KNIVES | CHUTE | HUNGER | GRUBWORMS |
|---|---|---|---|---|
| DEBORAH | KATIE | PAULSEN | LIGHTNING | MOSQUITOES |
| BIRCH | ROBESON | FREE SPACE | BRANNOCK | NECKTIE |
| TWELVE | SEVEN | TIME | JACKET | BALLARD |
| RASPBERRIES | COOK | MAP | FIFTEEN | SURVIVAL |

The River

| WOOD | TENSION | CANOE | BRIEFCASE | BOUGHS |
|---|---|---|---|---|
| RADIO | COUNSELOR | RAFT | FIRE | COMA |
| POPLAR | ETHICS | FREE SPACE | BEAVERS | TWO |
| FOOD | SIX | HOLTZER | SURVIVAL | FIFTEEN |
| MAP | COOK | RASPBERRIES | BALLARD | JACKET |

The River

| KATIE | MAP | GRUBWORMS | HOLTZER | BEAVERS |
|---|---|---|---|---|
| HUNGER | FOOD | BIRCH | COUNSELOR | PAULSEN |
| POPLAR | CHUTE | FREE SPACE | LIGHTNING | RAFT |
| WOOD | RASPBERRIES | FIFTEEN | BALLARD | MOSQUITOES |
| TWELVE | FLINT | BRIAN | COOK | JACKET |

The River

| CANOE | DEBORAH | TWO | TENSION | BOUGHS |
|---|---|---|---|---|
| SIX | ETHICS | NECKTIE | FIRE | BRANNOCK |
| COMA | BRIEFCASE | FREE SPACE | MANNERLY | ROBESON |
| SURVIVAL | TIME | SEVEN | JACKET | COOK |
| BRIAN | FLINT | TWELVE | MOSQUITOES | BALLARD |

## The River

| BRIEFCASE | WOOD | RADIO | RAFT | ROBESON |
| --- | --- | --- | --- | --- |
| BIRCH | TIME | FIFTEEN | SIX | RASPBERRIES |
| CANOE | MOSQUITOES | FREE SPACE | KATIE | BRANNOCK |
| FOOD | SEVEN | BRIAN | FIRE | ETHICS |
| HOLTZER | PAULSEN | MANNERLY | BOUGHS | BEAVERS |

## The River

| KNIVES | FLINT | TWELVE | NECKTIE | TENSION |
| --- | --- | --- | --- | --- |
| BALLARD | HUNGER | COUNSELOR | LIGHTNING | DEBORAH |
| COOK | MAP | FREE SPACE | SURVIVAL | POPLAR |
| TWO | GRUBWORMS | COMA | BEAVERS | BOUGHS |
| MANNERLY | PAULSEN | HOLTZER | ETHICS | FIRE |

The River

| BRANNOCK | JACKET | ROBESON | PAULSEN | RAFT |
|---|---|---|---|---|
| LIGHTNING | BEAVERS | MOSQUITOES | TIME | FIFTEEN |
| BOUGHS | DEBORAH | FREE SPACE | BRIEFCASE | CHUTE |
| COOK | BRIAN | MANNERLY | WOOD | FIRE |
| SEVEN | ETHICS | BIRCH | COUNSELOR | FLINT |

The River

| CANOE | HOLTZER | HUNGER | KATIE | RADIO |
|---|---|---|---|---|
| FOOD | MAP | POPLAR | TENSION | SIX |
| RASPBERRIES | TWELVE | FREE SPACE | NECKTIE | GRUBWORMS |
| SURVIVAL | COMA | KNIVES | FLINT | COUNSELOR |
| BIRCH | ETHICS | SEVEN | FIRE | WOOD |

The River

| CANOE | TIME | TENSION | COUNSELOR | KATIE |
|---|---|---|---|---|
| RASPBERRIES | SURVIVAL | SIX | COOK | HUNGER |
| FIRE | MOSQUITOES | FREE SPACE | SEVEN | HOLTZER |
| WOOD | KNIVES | MAP | LIGHTNING | MANNERLY |
| BALLARD | BRANNOCK | PAULSEN | COMA | TWELVE |

The River

| TWO | FIFTEEN | ETHICS | POPLAR | NECKTIE |
|---|---|---|---|---|
| GRUBWORMS | BRIEFCASE | FOOD | RAFT | RADIO |
| BIRCH | BOUGHS | FREE SPACE | BEAVERS | CHUTE |
| ROBESON | JACKET | FLINT | TWELVE | COMA |
| PAULSEN | BRANNOCK | BALLARD | MANNERLY | LIGHTNING |

The River

| NECKTIE | BALLARD | CANOE | BRIAN | JACKET |
|---|---|---|---|---|
| TWELVE | TWO | BIRCH | SEVEN | BRANNOCK |
| FLINT | FOOD | FREE SPACE | SURVIVAL | CHUTE |
| POPLAR | WOOD | ETHICS | ROBESON | COOK |
| MANNERLY | COMA | HOLTZER | MOSQUITOES | RAFT |

The River

| SIX | KNIVES | GRUBWORMS | COUNSELOR | DEBORAH |
|---|---|---|---|---|
| TIME | RADIO | KATIE | BOUGHS | BRIEFCASE |
| BEAVERS | HUNGER | FREE SPACE | TENSION | RASPBERRIES |
| LIGHTNING | FIFTEEN | MAP | RAFT | MOSQUITOES |
| HOLTZER | COMA | MANNERLY | COOK | ROBESON |

The River

| GRUBWORMS | TWO | TWELVE | BALLARD | RADIO |
|---|---|---|---|---|
| FLINT | SIX | ROBESON | KNIVES | BEAVERS |
| FIRE | CANOE | FREE SPACE | RASPBERRIES | LIGHTNING |
| RAFT | DEBORAH | POPLAR | NECKTIE | FOOD |
| BRIAN | HUNGER | CHUTE | BRANNOCK | BOUGHS |

The River

| JACKET | MANNERLY | KATIE | TENSION | MAP |
|---|---|---|---|---|
| SEVEN | WOOD | PAULSEN | BRIEFCASE | HOLTZER |
| BIRCH | SURVIVAL | FREE SPACE | TIME | COMA |
| COUNSELOR | MOSQUITOES | ETHICS | BOUGHS | BRANNOCK |
| CHUTE | HUNGER | BRIAN | FOOD | NECKTIE |

The River

| ROBESON | GRUBWORMS | SEVEN | TWELVE | RASPBERRIES |
|---|---|---|---|---|
| KATIE | RAFT | BIRCH | POPLAR | CANOE |
| NECKTIE | SIX | FREE SPACE | COOK | FIFTEEN |
| BOUGHS | PAULSEN | FOOD | FLINT | MOSQUITOES |
| WOOD | BALLARD | TIME | BRIEFCASE | COUNSELOR |

The River

| MAP | BRANNOCK | KNIVES | BEAVERS | RADIO |
|---|---|---|---|---|
| MANNERLY | COMA | LIGHTNING | JACKET | BRIAN |
| HOLTZER | CHUTE | FREE SPACE | TWO | SURVIVAL |
| TENSION | HUNGER | FIRE | COUNSELOR | BRIEFCASE |
| TIME | BALLARD | WOOD | MOSQUITOES | FLINT |

The River

| BRANNOCK | CHUTE | KATIE | COUNSELOR | BOUGHS |
|---|---|---|---|---|
| POPLAR | TWO | BIRCH | TENSION | SEVEN |
| GRUBWORMS | SURVIVAL | FREE SPACE | DEBORAH | BEAVERS |
| MOSQUITOES | FIRE | NECKTIE | MAP | TWELVE |
| SIX | KNIVES | FIFTEEN | COMA | HOLTZER |

The River

| LIGHTNING | HUNGER | BRIAN | JACKET | BALLARD |
|---|---|---|---|---|
| CANOE | BRIEFCASE | ROBESON | RASPBERRIES | FLINT |
| WOOD | RAFT | FREE SPACE | RADIO | PAULSEN |
| TIME | COOK | MANNERLY | HOLTZER | COMA |
| FIFTEEN | KNIVES | SIX | TWELVE | MAP |

The River

| RAFT | SEVEN | GRUBWORMS | ETHICS | FIRE |
|---|---|---|---|---|
| SIX | KNIVES | CHUTE | TWO | HUNGER |
| MAP | FOOD | FREE SPACE | SURVIVAL | BEAVERS |
| FLINT | COOK | POPLAR | BRIAN | DEBORAH |
| TIME | ROBESON | CANOE | BRANNOCK | RASPBERRIES |

The River

| FIFTEEN | COUNSELOR | NECKTIE | JACKET | BIRCH |
|---|---|---|---|---|
| COMA | BRIEFCASE | RADIO | KATIE | TENSION |
| BOUGHS | MOSQUITOES | FREE SPACE | LIGHTNING | PAULSEN |
| HOLTZER | WOOD | TWELVE | RASPBERRIES | BRANNOCK |
| CANOE | ROBESON | TIME | DEBORAH | BRIAN |

The River

| GRUBWORMS | FLINT | TWELVE | KATIE | WOOD |
|---|---|---|---|---|
| FOOD | NECKTIE | SURVIVAL | COUNSELOR | KNIVES |
| BRIAN | BRIEFCASE | FREE SPACE | PAULSEN | ETHICS |
| TENSION | SEVEN | COMA | CANOE | FIRE |
| MOSQUITOES | RADIO | ROBESON | COOK | RAFT |

The River

| BIRCH | BOUGHS | SIX | FIFTEEN | POPLAR |
|---|---|---|---|---|
| TIME | CHUTE | DEBORAH | MANNERLY | BALLARD |
| LIGHTNING | BEAVERS | FREE SPACE | MAP | RASPBERRIES |
| JACKET | BRANNOCK | HUNGER | RAFT | COOK |
| ROBESON | RADIO | MOSQUITOES | FIRE | CANOE |

The River

| COMA | TENSION | TWELVE | DEBORAH | RASPBERRIES |
|---|---|---|---|---|
| SEVEN | COUNSELOR | FLINT | COOK | JACKET |
| CANOE | MANNERLY | FREE SPACE | POPLAR | WOOD |
| GRUBWORMS | FOOD | RADIO | KATIE | BRIAN |
| MOSQUITOES | TWO | RAFT | SURVIVAL | BIRCH |

The River

| BRIEFCASE | PAULSEN | BALLARD | ETHICS | NECKTIE |
|---|---|---|---|---|
| TIME | SIX | FIRE | MAP | HUNGER |
| BRANNOCK | FIFTEEN | FREE SPACE | KNIVES | BEAVERS |
| HOLTZER | ROBESON | BOUGHS | BIRCH | SURVIVAL |
| RAFT | TWO | MOSQUITOES | BRIAN | KATIE |

**River Vocabulary Word List**

| No. | Word | Clue/Definition |
|---|---|---|
| 1. | ACCURATE | Exact |
| 2. | ALCOVE | An indentation or small hollow |
| 3. | ANVIL | Heavy block of iron or steel |
| 4. | ASPECT | Way of looking at something |
| 5. | BUFFETED | Hit; beat |
| 6. | CAREENING | Rushing headlong |
| 7. | CHUTE | A waterfall; a channel |
| 8. | CLAMBERED | Climbed |
| 9. | COMA | Unconsciousness |
| 10. | COMPROMISE | Agreement |
| 11. | CRUDE | Roughly made |
| 12. | CUE | Sign |
| 13. | DEHYDRATION | Loss of water or moisture |
| 14. | DISINTEGRATE | To fall apart |
| 15. | DOUBTS | Uncertainties |
| 16. | EMBEDDED | Firmly enclosed |
| 17. | ENHANCED | Improved |
| 18. | EVASIVE | Misleading; avoiding |
| 19. | EXASPERATION | Annoyance |
| 20. | EXTERNALIZE | To show outwardly |
| 21. | FEND | Fight against |
| 22. | FLEXED | Bent |
| 23. | GLAZED | Glassy-eyed |
| 24. | HORDE | A large group; swarm |
| 25. | INDICATION | Sign; signal |
| 26. | LURCHED | Rolled; dipped down |
| 27. | MAROONED | Abandoned |
| 28. | MASSIVE | Enormous |
| 29. | MUTED | Muffled; softened |
| 30. | NEGATED | Ruled out |
| 31. | PERVERSELY | Wrongly stubborn |
| 32. | PRECAUTION | Safeguard |
| 33. | PRYING | Looking curiously; snooping |
| 34. | PULVERIZED | Ground to powder or dust |
| 35. | RECTIFY | To set right; correct |
| 36. | RELENTED | Eased off |
| 37. | REVERT | To return to a former condition |
| 38. | SKIMPY | Not enough; inadequate |
| 39. | SQUELCH | To silence |
| 40. | STABLE | Sturdy |
| 41. | STUNNED | Shocked |
| 42. | SUBMERGED | Covered with water |
| 43. | THRIVE | Succeed |
| 44. | VETOED | Rejected; refused |
| 45. | VOWED | Promised |

River Vocabulary Fill In The Blanks 1

_____  1. To show outwardly
_____  2. Sign
_____  3. Climbed
_____  4. Unconsciousness
_____  5. To set right; correct
_____  6. Promised
_____  7. Ruled out
_____  8. Sturdy
_____  9. Agreement
_____  10. Misleading; avoiding
_____  11. Abandoned
_____  12. Uncertainties
_____  13. Succeed
_____  14. Annoyance
_____  15. To return to a former condition
_____  16. Firmly enclosed
_____  17. Covered with water
_____  18. Rolled; dipped down
_____  19. Rejected; refused
_____  20. A large group; swarm

River Vocabulary Fill In The Blanks 1 Answer Key

| | |
|---|---|
| EXTERNALIZE | 1. To show outwardly |
| CUE | 2. Sign |
| CLAMBERED | 3. Climbed |
| COMA | 4. Unconsciousness |
| RECTIFY | 5. To set right; correct |
| VOWED | 6. Promised |
| NEGATED | 7. Ruled out |
| STABLE | 8. Sturdy |
| COMPROMISE | 9. Agreement |
| EVASIVE | 10. Misleading; avoiding |
| MAROONED | 11. Abandoned |
| DOUBTS | 12. Uncertainties |
| THRIVE | 13. Succeed |
| EXASPERATION | 14. Annoyance |
| REVERT | 15. To return to a former condition |
| EMBEDDED | 16. Firmly enclosed |
| SUBMERGED | 17. Covered with water |
| LURCHED | 18. Rolled; dipped down |
| VETOED | 19. Rejected; refused |
| HORDE | 20. A large group; swarm |

River Vocabulary Fill In The Blanks 2

_____  1. Glassy-eyed
_____  2. Abandoned
_____  3. To show outwardly
_____  4. Sturdy
_____  5. Promised
_____  6. Way of looking at something
_____  7. To silence
_____  8. A waterfall; a channel
_____  9. Improved
_____  10. To return to a former condition
_____  11. To set right; correct
_____  12. Muffled; softened
_____  13. Ground to powder or dust
_____  14. Sign
_____  15. To fall apart
_____  16. Misleading; avoiding
_____  17. A large group; swarm
_____  18. Annoyance
_____  19. Safeguard
_____  20. Fight against

River Vocabulary Fill In The Blanks 2 Answer Key

| | |
|---|---|
| GLAZED | 1. Glassy-eyed |
| MAROONED | 2. Abandoned |
| EXTERNALIZE | 3. To show outwardly |
| STABLE | 4. Sturdy |
| VOWED | 5. Promised |
| ASPECT | 6. Way of looking at something |
| SQUELCH | 7. To silence |
| CHUTE | 8. A waterfall; a channel |
| ENHANCED | 9. Improved |
| REVERT | 10. To return to a former condition |
| RECTIFY | 11. To set right; correct |
| MUTED | 12. Muffled; softened |
| PULVERIZED | 13. Ground to powder or dust |
| CUE | 14. Sign |
| DISINTEGRATE | 15. To fall apart |
| EVASIVE | 16. Misleading; avoiding |
| HORDE | 17. A large group; swarm |
| EXASPERATION | 18. Annoyance |
| PRECAUTION | 19. Safeguard |
| FEND | 20. Fight against |

River Vocabulary Fill In The Blanks 3

_____  1. To show outwardly
_____  2. To silence
_____  3. Uncertainties
_____  4. Shocked
_____  5. Sturdy
_____  6. Unconsciousness
_____  7. Rejected; refused
_____  8. A waterfall; a channel
_____  9. Enormous
_____ 10. Safeguard
_____ 11. Loss of water or moisture
_____ 12. Way of looking at something
_____ 13. Eased off
_____ 14. An indentation or small hollow
_____ 15. Rushing headlong
_____ 16. Muffled; softened
_____ 17. Rolled; dipped down
_____ 18. Promised
_____ 19. Roughly made
_____ 20. Looking curiously; snooping

River Vocabulary Fill In The Blanks 3 Answer Key

| | |
|---|---|
| EXTERNALIZE | 1. To show outwardly |
| SQUELCH | 2. To silence |
| DOUBTS | 3. Uncertainties |
| STUNNED | 4. Shocked |
| STABLE | 5. Sturdy |
| COMA | 6. Unconsciousness |
| VETOED | 7. Rejected; refused |
| CHUTE | 8. A waterfall; a channel |
| MASSIVE | 9. Enormous |
| PRECAUTION | 10. Safeguard |
| DEHYDRATION | 11. Loss of water or moisture |
| ASPECT | 12. Way of looking at something |
| RELENTED | 13. Eased off |
| ALCOVE | 14. An indentation or small hollow |
| CAREENING | 15. Rushing headlong |
| MUTED | 16. Muffled; softened |
| LURCHED | 17. Rolled; dipped down |
| VOWED | 18. Promised |
| CRUDE | 19. Roughly made |
| PRYING | 20. Looking curiously; snooping |

River Vocabulary Fill In The Blanks 4

_____   1. Ruled out
_____   2. Heavy block of iron or steel
_____   3. Fight against
_____   4. Sign; signal
_____   5. Succeed
_____   6. Rejected; refused
_____   7. Way of looking at something
_____   8. Roughly made
_____   9. Bent
_____   10. Muffled; softened
_____   11. Misleading; avoiding
_____   12. Eased off
_____   13. Improved
_____   14. Covered with water
_____   15. A waterfall; a channel
_____   16. Rolled; dipped down
_____   17. To return to a former condition
_____   18. Climbed
_____   19. Enormous
_____   20. Abandoned

River Vocabulary Fill In The Blanks 4 Answer Key

| | |
|---|---|
| NEGATED | 1. Ruled out |
| ANVIL | 2. Heavy block of iron or steel |
| FEND | 3. Fight against |
| INDICATION | 4. Sign; signal |
| THRIVE | 5. Succeed |
| VETOED | 6. Rejected; refused |
| ASPECT | 7. Way of looking at something |
| CRUDE | 8. Roughly made |
| FLEXED | 9. Bent |
| MUTED | 10. Muffled; softened |
| EVASIVE | 11. Misleading; avoiding |
| RELENTED | 12. Eased off |
| ENHANCED | 13. Improved |
| SUBMERGED | 14. Covered with water |
| CHUTE | 15. A waterfall; a channel |
| LURCHED | 16. Rolled; dipped down |
| REVERT | 17. To return to a former condition |
| CLAMBERED | 18. Climbed |
| MASSIVE | 19. Enormous |
| MAROONED | 20. Abandoned |

River Vocabulary Matching 1

___ 1. MAROONED          A. Rejected; refused
___ 2. PULVERIZED         B. A waterfall; a channel
___ 3. EXASPERATION       C. Unconsciousness
___ 4. PRECAUTION         D. Heavy block of iron or steel
___ 5. CLAMBERED          E. Rushing headlong
___ 6. BUFFETED           F. Rolled; dipped down
___ 7. CAREENING          G. Annoyance
___ 8. ASPECT             H. Muffled; softened
___ 9. STUNNED            I. Abandoned
___10. COMA               J. To silence
___11. DISINTEGRATE       K. Shocked
___12. DEHYDRATION        L. To return to a former condition
___13. REVERT             M. Loss of water or moisture
___14. RELENTED           N. Hit; beat
___15. LURCHED            O. Climbed
___16. VETOED             P. Bent
___17. SQUELCH            Q. Fight against
___18. MUTED              R. Sign
___19. THRIVE             S. Eased off
___20. ANVIL              T. To fall apart
___21. CUE                U. Safeguard
___22. FLEXED             V. Misleading; avoiding
___23. EVASIVE            W. Succeed
___24. CHUTE              X. Ground to powder or dust
___25. FEND               Y. Way of looking at something

River Vocabulary Matching 1 Answer Key

| | | | |
|---|---|---|---|
| I - | 1. MAROONED | A. | Rejected; refused |
| X - | 2. PULVERIZED | B. | A waterfall; a channel |
| G - | 3. EXASPERATION | C. | Unconsciousness |
| U - | 4. PRECAUTION | D. | Heavy block of iron or steel |
| O - | 5. CLAMBERED | E. | Rushing headlong |
| N - | 6. BUFFETED | F. | Rolled; dipped down |
| E - | 7. CAREENING | G. | Annoyance |
| Y - | 8. ASPECT | H. | Muffled; softened |
| K - | 9. STUNNED | I. | Abandoned |
| C - | 10. COMA | J. | To silence |
| T - | 11. DISINTEGRATE | K. | Shocked |
| M - | 12. DEHYDRATION | L. | To return to a former condition |
| L - | 13. REVERT | M. | Loss of water or moisture |
| S - | 14. RELENTED | N. | Hit; beat |
| F - | 15. LURCHED | O. | Climbed |
| A - | 16. VETOED | P. | Bent |
| J - | 17. SQUELCH | Q. | Fight against |
| H - | 18. MUTED | R. | Sign |
| W - | 19. THRIVE | S. | Eased off |
| D - | 20. ANVIL | T. | To fall apart |
| R - | 21. CUE | U. | Safeguard |
| P - | 22. FLEXED | V. | Misleading; avoiding |
| V - | 23. EVASIVE | W. | Succeed |
| B - | 24. CHUTE | X. | Ground to powder or dust |
| Q - | 25. FEND | Y. | Way of looking at something |

River Vocabulary Matching 2

___ 1. STABLE           A. Sign
___ 2. VOWED            B. Abandoned
___ 3. GLAZED           C. Firmly enclosed
___ 4. HORDE            D. Ruled out
___ 5. EVASIVE          E. Annoyance
___ 6. BUFFETED         F. Looking curiously; snooping
___ 7. EXASPERATION     G. A large group; swarm
___ 8. PULVERIZED       H. Misleading; avoiding
___ 9. PRYING           I. Not enough; inadequate
___ 10. RELENTED        J. Promised
___ 11. DEHYDRATION     K. Exact
___ 12. CHUTE           L. Covered with water
___ 13. DOUBTS          M. Sturdy
___ 14. SKIMPY          N. Fight against
___ 15. DISINTEGRATE    O. Ground to powder or dust
___ 16. CUE             P. To fall apart
___ 17. CLAMBERED       Q. Glassy-eyed
___ 18. EMBEDDED        R. Uncertainties
___ 19. MAROONED        S. Climbed
___ 20. NEGATED         T. To silence
___ 21. STUNNED         U. Eased off
___ 22. FEND            V. Loss of water or moisture
___ 23. SQUELCH         W. Shocked
___ 24. SUBMERGED       X. Hit; beat
___ 25. ACCURATE        Y. A waterfall; a channel

River Vocabulary Matching 2 Answer Key

| | | |
|---|---|---|
| M - 1. STABLE | A. Sign |
| J - 2. VOWED | B. Abandoned |
| Q - 3. GLAZED | C. Firmly enclosed |
| G - 4. HORDE | D. Ruled out |
| H - 5. EVASIVE | E. Annoyance |
| X - 6. BUFFETED | F. Looking curiously; snooping |
| E - 7. EXASPERATION | G. A large group; swarm |
| O - 8. PULVERIZED | H. Misleading; avoiding |
| F - 9. PRYING | I. Not enough; inadequate |
| U - 10. RELENTED | J. Promised |
| V - 11. DEHYDRATION | K. Exact |
| Y - 12. CHUTE | L. Covered with water |
| R - 13. DOUBTS | M. Sturdy |
| I - 14. SKIMPY | N. Fight against |
| P - 15. DISINTEGRATE | O. Ground to powder or dust |
| A - 16. CUE | P. To fall apart |
| S - 17. CLAMBERED | Q. Glassy-eyed |
| C - 18. EMBEDDED | R. Uncertainties |
| B - 19. MAROONED | S. Climbed |
| D - 20. NEGATED | T. To silence |
| W - 21. STUNNED | U. Eased off |
| N - 22. FEND | V. Loss of water or moisture |
| T - 23. SQUELCH | W. Shocked |
| L - 24. SUBMERGED | X. Hit; beat |
| K - 25. ACCURATE | Y. A waterfall; a channel |

River Vocabulary Matching 3

___ 1. SKIMPY          A. Loss of water or moisture
___ 2. CUE             B. Not enough; inadequate
___ 3. ACCURATE        C. Abandoned
___ 4. MASSIVE         D. Unconsciousness
___ 5. BUFFETED        E. Rolled; dipped down
___ 6. ENHANCED        F. A waterfall; a channel
___ 7. HORDE           G. Hit; beat
___ 8. COMPROMISE      H. Enormous
___ 9. PERVERSELY      I. Wrongly stubborn
___10. RECTIFY         J. To set right; correct
___11. FEND            K. To fall apart
___12. SQUELCH         L. Safeguard
___13. DEHYDRATION     M. Exact
___14. ALCOVE          N. Firmly enclosed
___15. EMBEDDED        O. Covered with water
___16. SUBMERGED       P. Rejected; refused
___17. PRECAUTION      Q. Glassy-eyed
___18. COMA            R. Agreement
___19. GLAZED          S. To show outwardly
___20. MAROONED        T. Improved
___21. VETOED          U. An indentation or small hollow
___22. EXTERNALIZE     V. Sign
___23. LURCHED         W. To silence
___24. DISINTEGRATE    X. A large group; swarm
___25. CHUTE           Y. Fight against

River Vocabulary Matching 3 Answer Key

| | | | |
|---|---|---|---|
| B - 1. SKIMPY | A. Loss of water or moisture |
| V - 2. CUE | B. Not enough; inadequate |
| M - 3. ACCURATE | C. Abandoned |
| H - 4. MASSIVE | D. Unconsciousness |
| G - 5. BUFFETED | E. Rolled; dipped down |
| T - 6. ENHANCED | F. A waterfall; a channel |
| X - 7. HORDE | G. Hit; beat |
| R - 8. COMPROMISE | H. Enormous |
| I - 9. PERVERSELY | I. Wrongly stubborn |
| J - 10. RECTIFY | J. To set right; correct |
| Y - 11. FEND | K. To fall apart |
| W - 12. SQUELCH | L. Safeguard |
| A - 13. DEHYDRATION | M. Exact |
| U - 14. ALCOVE | N. Firmly enclosed |
| N - 15. EMBEDDED | O. Covered with water |
| O - 16. SUBMERGED | P. Rejected; refused |
| L - 17. PRECAUTION | Q. Glassy-eyed |
| D - 18. COMA | R. Agreement |
| Q - 19. GLAZED | S. To show outwardly |
| C - 20. MAROONED | T. Improved |
| P - 21. VETOED | U. An indentation or small hollow |
| S - 22. EXTERNALIZE | V. Sign |
| E - 23. LURCHED | W. To silence |
| K - 24. DISINTEGRATE | X. A large group; swarm |
| F - 25. CHUTE | Y. Fight against |

Copyrighted

River Vocabulary Matching 4

___ 1. HORDE  A. A waterfall; a channel
___ 2. CAREENING  B. Sign; signal
___ 3. THRIVE  C. Covered with water
___ 4. CLAMBERED  D. A large group; swarm
___ 5. RECTIFY  E. Rejected; refused
___ 6. SUBMERGED  F. Not enough; inadequate
___ 7. FLEXED  G. Looking curiously; snooping
___ 8. SKIMPY  H. Misleading; avoiding
___ 9. EMBEDDED  I. Abandoned
___10. FEND  J. To fall apart
___11. VOWED  K. An indentation or small hollow
___12. INDICATION  L. Fight against
___13. MAROONED  M. Promised
___14. PRYING  N. Annoyance
___15. DISINTEGRATE  O. To set right; correct
___16. EVASIVE  P. Uncertainties
___17. ALCOVE  Q. Succeed
___18. VETOED  R. Climbed
___19. COMA  S. Muffled; softened
___20. ENHANCED  T. Rushing headlong
___21. EXASPERATION  U. Unconsciousness
___22. MUTED  V. Firmly enclosed
___23. CHUTE  W. Bent
___24. RELENTED  X. Eased off
___25. DOUBTS  Y. Improved

River Vocabulary Matching 4 Answer Key

| | | | |
|---|---|---|---|
| D - 1. | HORDE | A. | A waterfall; a channel |
| T - 2. | CAREENING | B. | Sign; signal |
| Q - 3. | THRIVE | C. | Covered with water |
| R - 4. | CLAMBERED | D. | A large group; swarm |
| O - 5. | RECTIFY | E. | Rejected; refused |
| C - 6. | SUBMERGED | F. | Not enough; inadequate |
| W - 7. | FLEXED | G. | Looking curiously; snooping |
| F - 8. | SKIMPY | H. | Misleading; avoiding |
| V - 9. | EMBEDDED | I. | Abandoned |
| L - 10. | FEND | J. | To fall apart |
| M - 11. | VOWED | K. | An indentation or small hollow |
| B - 12. | INDICATION | L. | Fight against |
| I - 13. | MAROONED | M. | Promised |
| G - 14. | PRYING | N. | Annoyance |
| J - 15. | DISINTEGRATE | O. | To set right; correct |
| H - 16. | EVASIVE | P. | Uncertainties |
| K - 17. | ALCOVE | Q. | Succeed |
| E - 18. | VETOED | R. | Climbed |
| U - 19. | COMA | S. | Muffled; softened |
| Y - 20. | ENHANCED | T. | Rushing headlong |
| N - 21. | EXASPERATION | U. | Unconsciousness |
| S - 22. | MUTED | V. | Firmly enclosed |
| A - 23. | CHUTE | W. | Bent |
| X - 24. | RELENTED | X. | Eased off |
| P - 25. | DOUBTS | Y. | Improved |

River Vocabulary Magic Squares 1

Match the definition with the vocabulary word. Put your answers in the magic squares below. When your answers are correct, all columns and rows will add to the same number.

A. STABLE
B. PRECAUTION
C. SKIMPY
D. BUFFETED
E. COMPROMISE
F. COMA
G. PRYING
H. ALCOVE
I. THRIVE
J. CRUDE
K. ASPECT
L. CAREENING
M. GLAZED
N. REVERT
O. LURCHED
P. DOUBTS

1. Rolled; dipped down
2. Hit; beat
3. Roughly made
4. Agreement
5. Succeed
6. Unconsciousness
7. Uncertainties
8. Not enough; inadequate
9. An indentation or small hollow
10. Way of looking at something
11. Sturdy
12. To return to a former condition
13. Safeguard
14. Glassy-eyed
15. Looking curiously; snooping
16. Rushing headlong

| A= | B= | C= | D= |
| E= | F= | G= | H= |
| I= | J= | K= | L= |
| M= | N= | O= | P= |

River Vocabulary Magic Squares 1 Answer Key

Match the definition with the vocabulary word. Put your answers in the magic squares below. When your answers are correct, all columns and rows will add to the same number.

A. STABLE
B. PRECAUTION
C. SKIMPY
D. BUFFETED
E. COMPROMISE
F. COMA
G. PRYING
H. ALCOVE
I. THRIVE
J. CRUDE
K. ASPECT
L. CAREENING
M. GLAZED
N. REVERT
O. LURCHED
P. DOUBTS

1. Rolled; dipped down
2. Hit; beat
3. Roughly made
4. Agreement
5. Succeed
6. Unconsciousness
7. Uncertainties
8. Not enough; inadequate
9. An indentation or small hollow
10. Way of looking at something
11. Sturdy
12. To return to a former condition
13. Safeguard
14. Glassy-eyed
15. Looking curiously; snooping
16. Rushing headlong

| A=11 | B=13 | C=8 | D=2 |
| --- | --- | --- | --- |
| E=4 | F=6 | G=15 | H=9 |
| I=5 | J=3 | K=10 | L=16 |
| M=14 | N=12 | O=1 | P=7 |

River Vocabulary Magic Squares 2

Match the definition with the vocabulary word. Put your answers in the magic squares below. When your answers are correct, all columns and rows will add to the same number.

A. RELENTED
B. DEHYDRATION
C. PULVERIZED
D. COMA
E. PRYING
F. VETOED
G. ACCURATE
H. NEGATED
I. CAREENING
J. GLAZED
K. EMBEDDED
L. BUFFETED
M. CRUDE
N. PERVERSELY
O. COMPROMISE
P. RECTIFY

1. Loss of water or moisture
2. Exact
3. Firmly enclosed
4. Wrongly stubborn
5. Roughly made
6. Hit; beat
7. Ruled out
8. Eased off
9. To set right; correct
10. Rushing headlong
11. Looking curiously; snooping
12. Unconsciousness
13. Ground to powder or dust
14. Rejected; refused
15. Glassy-eyed
16. Agreement

| A= | B= | C= | D= |
| E= | F= | G= | H= |
| I= | J= | K= | L= |
| M= | N= | O= | P= |

River Vocabulary Magic Squares 2 Answer Key

Match the definition with the vocabulary word. Put your answers in the magic squares below. When your answers are correct, all columns and rows will add to the same number.

| | | | |
|---|---|---|---|
| A. RELENTED | E. PRYING | I. CAREENING | M. CRUDE |
| B. DEHYDRATION | F. VETOED | J. GLAZED | N. PERVERSELY |
| C. PULVERIZED | G. ACCURATE | K. EMBEDDED | O. COMPROMISE |
| D. COMA | H. NEGATED | L. BUFFETED | P. RECTIFY |

1. Loss of water or moisture
2. Exact
3. Firmly enclosed
4. Wrongly stubborn
5. Roughly made
6. Hit; beat
7. Ruled out
8. Eased off
9. To set right; correct
10. Rushing headlong
11. Looking curiously; snooping
12. Unconsciousness
13. Ground to powder or dust
14. Rejected; refused
15. Glassy-eyed
16. Agreement

| A=8 | B=1 | C=13 | D=12 |
|---|---|---|---|
| E=11 | F=14 | G=2 | H=7 |
| I=10 | J=15 | K=3 | L=6 |
| M=5 | N=4 | O=16 | P=9 |

River Vocabulary Magic Squares 3

Match the definition with the vocabulary word. Put your answers in the magic squares below. When your answers are correct, all columns and rows will add to the same number.

A. PERVERSELY   E. REVERT       I. SKIMPY       M. RELENTED
B. STUNNED      F. HORDE        J. DOUBTS       N. ACCURATE
C. PRECAUTION   G. BUFFETED     K. PULVERIZED   O. SQUELCH
D. DISINTEGRATE H. NEGATED      L. INDICATION   P. ASPECT

1. A large group; swarm
2. Not enough; inadequate
3. To silence
4. To fall apart
5. Eased off
6. Shocked
7. Ruled out
8. Ground to powder or dust
9. Safeguard
10. Way of looking at something
11. Uncertainties
12. To return to a former condition
13. Sign; signal
14. Hit; beat
15. Wrongly stubborn
16. Exact

| A= | B= | C= | D= |
| E= | F= | G= | H= |
| I= | J= | K= | L= |
| M= | N= | O= | P= |

82
Copyrighted

River Vocabulary Magic Squares 3 Answer Key

Match the definition with the vocabulary word. Put your answers in the magic squares below. When your answers are correct, all columns and rows will add to the same number.

A. PERVERSELY
B. STUNNED
C. PRECAUTION
D. DISINTEGRATE
E. REVERT
F. HORDE
G. BUFFETED
H. NEGATED
I. SKIMPY
J. DOUBTS
K. PULVERIZED
L. INDICATION
M. RELENTED
N. ACCURATE
O. SQUELCH
P. ASPECT

1. A large group; swarm
2. Not enough; inadequate
3. To silence
4. To fall apart
5. Eased off
6. Shocked
7. Ruled out
8. Ground to powder or dust
9. Safeguard
10. Way of looking at something
11. Uncertainties
12. To return to a former condition
13. Sign; signal
14. Hit; beat
15. Wrongly stubborn
16. Exact

| A=15 | B=6 | C=9 | D=4 |
| --- | --- | --- | --- |
| E=12 | F=1 | G=14 | H=7 |
| I=2 | J=11 | K=8 | L=13 |
| M=5 | N=16 | O=3 | P=10 |

River Vocabulary Magic Squares 4

Match the definition with the vocabulary word. Put your answers in the magic squares below. When your answers are correct, all columns and rows will add to the same number.

| | | | |
|---|---|---|---|
| A. BUFFETED | E. MASSIVE | I. ASPECT | M. PERVERSELY |
| B. SKIMPY | F. SUBMERGED | J. CUE | N. EXASPERATION |
| C. PULVERIZED | G. ALCOVE | K. FLEXED | O. INDICATION |
| D. VETOED | H. PRYING | L. CLAMBERED | P. ANVIL |

1. Annoyance
2. An indentation or small hollow
3. Climbed
4. Hit; beat
5. Bent
6. Not enough; inadequate
7. Wrongly stubborn
8. Looking curiously; snooping
9. Enormous
10. Heavy block of iron or steel
11. Ground to powder or dust
12. Sign
13. Rejected; refused
14. Way of looking at something
15. Covered with water
16. Sign; signal

| | | | |
|---|---|---|---|
| A= | B= | C= | D= |
| E= | F= | G= | H= |
| I= | J= | K= | L= |
| M= | N= | O= | P= |

84
Copyrighted

River Vocabulary Magic Squares 4 Answer Key

Match the definition with the vocabulary word. Put your answers in the magic squares below. When your answers are correct, all columns and rows will add to the same number.

A. BUFFETED
B. SKIMPY
C. PULVERIZED
D. VETOED
E. MASSIVE
F. SUBMERGED
G. ALCOVE
H. PRYING
I. ASPECT
J. CUE
K. FLEXED
L. CLAMBERED
M. PERVERSELY
N. EXASPERATION
O. INDICATION
P. ANVIL

1. Annoyance
2. An indentation or small hollow
3. Climbed
4. Hit; beat
5. Bent
6. Not enough; inadequate
7. Wrongly stubborn
8. Looking curiously; snooping
9. Enormous
10. Heavy block of iron or steel
11. Ground to powder or dust
12. Sign
13. Rejected; refused
14. Way of looking at something
15. Covered with water
16. Sign; signal

| A=4 | B=6 | C=11 | D=13 |
| --- | --- | --- | --- |
| E=9 | F=15 | G=2 | H=8 |
| I=14 | J=12 | K=5 | L=3 |
| M=7 | N=1 | O=16 | P=10 |

River Vocabulary Word Search 1

Words are placed backwards, forward, diagonally, up and down. Clues listed below can help you find the words. Circle the hidden vocabulary words in the maze.

```
S E V A S I V E T A R G E T N I S I D H
K W X Y Z T K D E S I M O R P M O C S H
I G V D R N H G G H M J Q N E P H L P H
M B D E X T E R N A L I Z E R U V A K L
P N U E S Z G F I V W W P G V L V M M G
Y Y N F H Q J P L V H G R A E V I B L V
Q L V H F Y U W F T E H E T R E N E M D
H Z Z R J E D E N S Y R C E S R D R F H
W B D R P T T R L Z W N A D E I I E T D
V K D S R W B E A C Q Q U M L Z C D C R
T M S E P W R Y D T H C T A Y E A D E S
V L V P F V E C D H I N I C L D T Y P H
H E W R G T C E A O D O O A N C I N S N
R S V Y J F T M A R O O N E D C O M A G
R S M I W U I B D D E V F U T I N V D T
C D C N M W F E H E I E K C T C M A E V
R H R G L N Y D F L V C N A R Q A C N M
E L U R C H E D W L E V R I M D S C N P
L J D T B X O E G L E E B N R S U U P
E K E K E U X D B L P X G T Z G I R T Z
N G W H B F J A V S A D E W O V V A S F
T Q C T T C T S A X B Z J D G E E T Q M
E B S D H S T X S U B M E R G E D E G X
D G Q Q V M E N H A N C E D Q T Q N F P
```

A large group; swarm (5)
A waterfall; a channel (5)
Abandoned (8)
Agreement (10)
An indentation or small hollow (6)
Annoyance (12)
Bent (6)
Climbed (9)
Covered with water (9)
Eased off (8)
Enormous (7)
Exact (8)
Fight against (4)
Firmly enclosed (8)
Glassy-eyed (6)
Ground to powder or dust (10)
Heavy block of iron or steel (5)
Hit; beat (8)
Improved (8)
Looking curiously; snooping (6)
Loss of water or moisture (11)
Misleading; avoiding (7)
Muffled; softened (5)

Not enough; inadequate (6)
Promised (5)
Rejected; refused (6)
Rolled; dipped down (7)
Roughly made (5)
Ruled out (7)
Rushing headlong (9)
Safeguard (10)
Shocked (7)
Sign (3)
Sign; signal (10)
Sturdy (6)
Succeed (6)
To fall apart (12)
To return to a former condition (6)
To set right; correct (7)
To show outwardly (11)
To silence (7)
Uncertainties (6)
Unconsciousness (4)
Way of looking at something (6)
Wrongly stubborn (10)

# River Vocabulary Word Search 1 Answer Key

Words are placed backwards, forward, diagonally, up and down. Clues listed below can help you find the words. Circle the hidden vocabulary words in the maze.

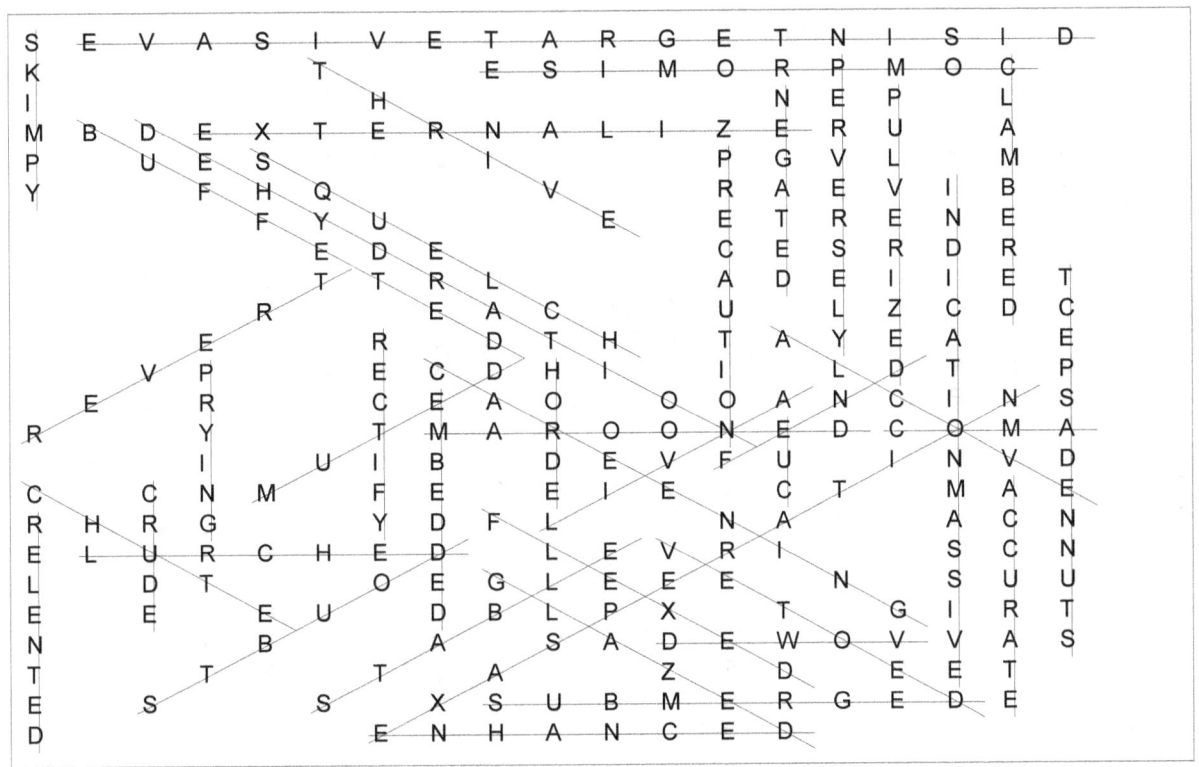

A large group; swarm (5)
A waterfall; a channel (5)
Abandoned (8)
Agreement (10)
An indentation or small hollow (6)
Annoyance (12)
Bent (6)
Climbed (9)
Covered with water (9)
Eased off (8)
Enormous (7)
Exact (8)
Fight against (4)
Firmly enclosed (8)
Glassy-eyed (6)
Ground to powder or dust (10)
Heavy block of iron or steel (5)
Hit; beat (8)
Improved (8)
Looking curiously; snooping (6)
Loss of water or moisture (11)
Misleading; avoiding (7)
Muffled; softened (5)

Not enough; inadequate (6)
Promised (5)
Rejected; refused (6)
Rolled; dipped down (7)
Roughly made (5)
Ruled out (7)
Rushing headlong (9)
Safeguard (10)
Shocked (7)
Sign (3)
Sign; signal (10)
Sturdy (6)
Succeed (6)
To fall apart (12)
To return to a former condition (6)
To set right; correct (7)
To show outwardly (11)
To silence (7)
Uncertainties (6)
Unconsciousness (4)
Way of looking at something (6)
Wrongly stubborn (10)

87
Copyrighted

River Vocabulary Word Search 2

Words are placed backwards, forward, diagonally, up and down. Clues listed below can help you find the words. Circle the hidden vocabulary words in the maze.

```
R E C T I F Y R S E S I M O R P M O C M
E N T J Z N L E K M P R E C A U T I O N
V T L G G T E L I B P U L V E R I Z E D
E Y Q C Z Y S E M E I N D I C A T I O N
R K N W W V R N P D K C Q J D G W J M K
T J V K C K E T Y D F R L D M J V X V G
H D P Z X A V E P E B V X A J Y J L G Y
F L E Y W V R D Y D F M S K M Q Q F M F
P K V H N G E E Q Z W A U P F B L L G L
B G G W Y E P Z E Q M R B V X F E K J E
J L E L T D G P W N D O M Q C H N R S X
M K V G F B R A M E I O E K H O Y L E E
E X A S P E R A T I O N R L U R C H E D
T N S V L V S E T E L E G E T D Q Z E M
Z R I C M S F F F I D D E N E E I T M V
Z Y V K I F E R P V O P D H J L U D S B
C U E V U A V O W E D N A A A M H O C G
S H E B G L I E S T W S M N Z C Z U R Z
T L K F L C R L H O P O R C L R Z B U P
U V B H A O H B M E C E V E V L S T D T
N J Z S Z V T A C D T W U D I P P S E X
N F J F E E B T S X C Q N V J M X P G S
E P C W D Z P S E Z S E N C N Q K B Q P
D A C C U R A T E Q F A P R Y I N G C V
```

A large group; swarm (5)
A waterfall; a channel (5)
Abandoned (8)
Agreement (10)
An indentation or small hollow (6)
Annoyance (12)
Bent (6)
Climbed (9)
Covered with water (9)
Eased off (8)
Enormous (7)
Exact (8)
Fight against (4)
Firmly enclosed (8)
Glassy-eyed (6)
Ground to powder or dust (10)
Heavy block of iron or steel (5)
Hit; beat (8)
Improved (8)
Looking curiously; snooping (6)
Loss of water or moisture (11)
Misleading; avoiding (7)
Muffled; softened (5)

Not enough; inadequate (6)
Promised (5)
Rejected; refused (6)
Rolled; dipped down (7)
Roughly made (5)
Ruled out (7)
Rushing headlong (9)
Safeguard (10)
Shocked (7)
Sign (3)
Sign; signal (10)
Sturdy (6)
Succeed (6)
To return to a former condition (6)
To set right; correct (7)
To show outwardly (11)
To silence (7)
Uncertainties (6)
Unconsciousness (4)
Way of looking at something (6)
Wrongly stubborn (10)

River Vocabulary Word Search 2 Answer Key

Words are placed backwards, forward, diagonally, up and down. Clues listed below can help you find the words. Circle the hidden vocabulary words in the maze.

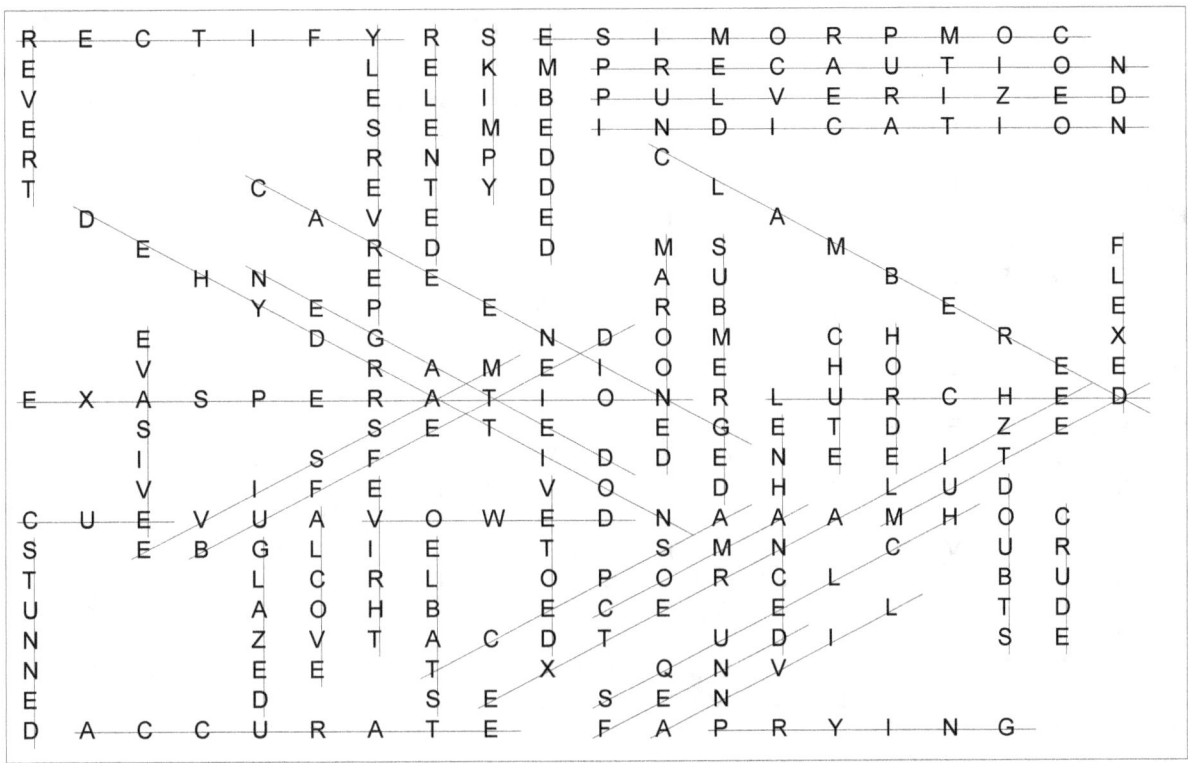

A large group; swarm (5)
A waterfall; a channel (5)
Abandoned (8)
Agreement (10)
An indentation or small hollow (6)
Annoyance (12)
Bent (6)
Climbed (9)
Covered with water (9)
Eased off (8)
Enormous (7)
Exact (8)
Fight against (4)
Firmly enclosed (8)
Glassy-eyed (6)
Ground to powder or dust (10)
Heavy block of iron or steel (5)
Hit; beat (8)
Improved (8)
Looking curiously; snooping (6)
Loss of water or moisture (11)
Misleading; avoiding (7)
Muffled; softened (5)

Not enough; inadequate (6)
Promised (5)
Rejected; refused (6)
Rolled; dipped down (7)
Roughly made (5)
Ruled out (7)
Rushing headlong (9)
Safeguard (10)
Shocked (7)
Sign (3)
Sign; signal (10)
Sturdy (6)
Succeed (6)
To return to a former condition (6)
To set right; correct (7)
To show outwardly (11)
To silence (7)
Uncertainties (6)
Unconsciousness (4)
Way of looking at something (6)
Wrongly stubborn (10)

River Vocabulary Word Search 3

Words are placed backwards, forward, diagonally, up and down. Words listed below are included in the maze. Circle the hidden vocabulary words in the maze.

```
B N L A L C O V E A S P E C T S F E M D
U E U N P R E C A U T I O N T T L M A T
F G R V B K X H A S Y M C B E A E B S T
F A C I D E N O O R A M U X F B X E S J
E T H L N R F G J X E O T M P L E D I R
T E E S F W C X X G D E N R L E D D V T
E D D L S R R N R R R W N B X B S E E K
D E T N E L E R R N S N M I M N F D N S
S H M T F D H P A S O U W G N B T P N Y
C D Y C R Z G L F I C W B N H G Y D S F
O R J O C D I B T N V H O M R X V M T S
M H H D S Z H A H B Y I B L E Y W K U M
P M D M E S R Q N L T E S S V R T Y N W
R K E B F E R E E A T L F P Q L G V N S
O B N C P X T S C A R N L U M U D E E D
M X H S Y A R I R Q P M D L P F E N D V
I Z A W R E D G N C P E Y V Z U Z L Z T
S X N U V N E P V R R R T E C F A V C V
E R C R I T M U T E D R Y R R P L O V H
N C E H N H S K B C T P B I E R G W D X
A P D I U Z L M S T M O G Z N V F E N N
Q P S F B T A N B I R D E E L G E D B L
X I V H P L E S K F C R U D E V I R H T
D K M F C Y C S T Y E V A S I V E B T M
```

| ACCURATE | COMPROMISE | EXTERNALIZE | MUTED | SKIMPY |
| ALCOVE | CRUDE | FEND | NEGATED | SQUELCH |
| ANVIL | CUE | FLEXED | PERVERSELY | STABLE |
| ASPECT | DISINTEGRATE | GLAZED | PRECAUTION | STUNNED |
| BUFFETED | DOUBTS | HORDE | PRYING | SUBMERGED |
| CAREENING | EMBEDDED | INDICATION | PULVERIZED | THRIVE |
| CHUTE | ENHANCED | LURCHED | RECTIFY | VETOED |
| CLAMBERED | EVASIVE | MAROONED | RELENTED | VOWED |
| COMA | EXASPERATION | MASSIVE | REVERT | |

River Vocabulary Word Search 3 Answer Key

Words are placed backwards, forward, diagonally, up and down. Words listed below are included in the maze. Circle the hidden vocabulary words in the maze.

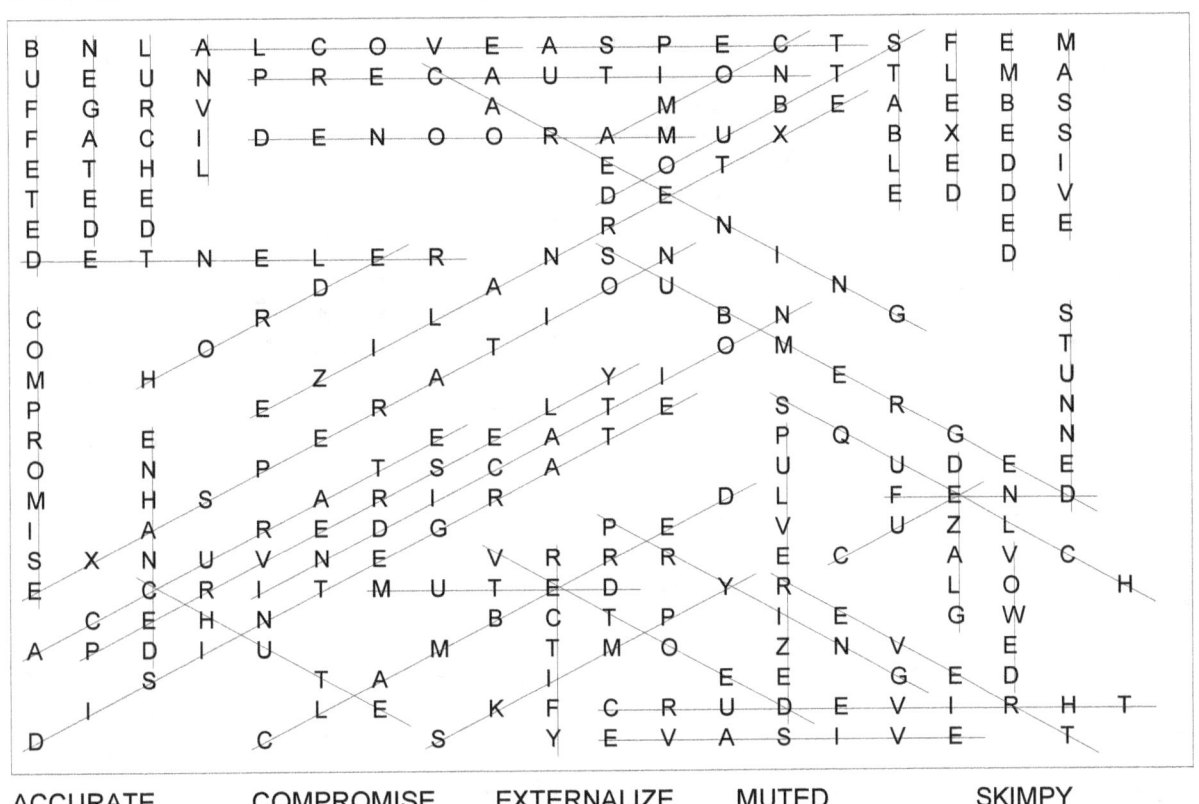

| ACCURATE | COMPROMISE | EXTERNALIZE | MUTED | SKIMPY |
| ALCOVE | CRUDE | FEND | NEGATED | SQUELCH |
| ANVIL | CUE | FLEXED | PERVERSELY | STABLE |
| ASPECT | DISINTEGRATE | GLAZED | PRECAUTION | STUNNED |
| BUFFETED | DOUBTS | HORDE | PRYING | SUBMERGED |
| CAREENING | EMBEDDED | INDICATION | PULVERIZED | THRIVE |
| CHUTE | ENHANCED | LURCHED | RECTIFY | VETOED |
| CLAMBERED | EVASIVE | MAROONED | RELENTED | VOWED |
| COMA | EXASPERATION | MASSIVE | REVERT | |

River Vocabulary Word Search 4

Words are placed backwards, forward, diagonally, up and down. Words listed below are included in the maze. Circle the hidden vocabulary words in the maze.

```
F  J  Z  D  D  E  C  N  A  H  N  E  S  T  U  N  N  E  D  P
J  L  F  Z  E  P  M  O  L  L  M  V  W  L  O  O  O  S  E  G
N  R  E  T  T  Z  Q  T  M  D  C  F  B  I  G  I  I  I  H  F
C  E  L  X  N  L  M  L  E  A  L  O  T  N  R  T  T  M  C  X
H  C  R  Q  E  V  R  N  E  R  D  U  V  D  D  A  A  O  R  B
U  T  R  B  L  D  O  V  N  E  A  G  D  E  S  R  C  R  U  C
T  I  Z  N  E  O  I  W  D  C  J  T  G  T  W  E  I  P  L  M
E  F  B  D  R  S  Y  D  E  R  N  R  X  E  H  P  D  M  W  H
K  Y  N  A  A  J  E  R  D  D  E  F  P  F  Q  S  N  O  V  H
L  E  M  V  S  B  P  B  S  M  J  Z  D  F  Y  A  I  C  X  B
F  D  E  M  M  S  S  B  B  D  N  F  C  U  T  X  N  D  R  S
C  E  F  E  Q  B  C  U  N  T  E  T  W  B  N  E  R  W  G  S
A  P  X  Q  Z  N  S  R  X  L  G  H  V  X  E  G  W  Z  L  R
R  C  R  T  Q  G  B  B  U  K  A  K  Y  H  V  J  G  C  D  L
E  L  S  V  E  S  M  Y  N  D  T  D  F  D  I  T  W  L  V  X
E  A  K  G  M  R  D  A  S  P  E  C  T  P  R  Y  I  N  G  N
N  M  I  Z  Q  T  N  G  C  T  D  W  Y  S  H  A  V  L  V  M
I  B  M  M  A  K  P  A  U  G  N  H  L  D  T  L  T  V  E  Z
N  E  P  J  S  N  P  M  L  G  Z  D  H  H  R  D  T  I  T  H
G  R  Y  P  U  L  V  E  R  I  Z  E  D  O  U  B  T  S  O  R
G  E  H  J  T  E  C  I  S  M  Z  H  P  Y  R  C  S  F  E  N
Q  D  M  M  S  U  B  M  L  D  V  E  H  F  K  D  Q  G  D  S
S  Q  U  E  L  C  H  G  L  A  Z  E  D  R  E  V  E  R  T  L
A  C  C  U  R  A  T  E  L  B  A  T  S  M  A  S  S  I  V  E
```

| ACCURATE | COMPROMISE | EXTERNALIZE | MUTED | SQUELCH |
| ALCOVE | CRUDE | FEND | NEGATED | STABLE |
| ANVIL | CUE | FLEXED | PRECAUTION | STUNNED |
| ASPECT | DEHYDRATION | GLAZED | PRYING | SUBMERGED |
| BUFFETED | DOUBTS | HORDE | PULVERIZED | THRIVE |
| CAREENING | EMBEDDED | INDICATION | RECTIFY | VETOED |
| CHUTE | ENHANCED | LURCHED | RELENTED | VOWED |
| CLAMBERED | EVASIVE | MAROONED | REVERT | |
| COMA | EXASPERATION | MASSIVE | SKIMPY | |

River Vocabulary Word Search 4 Answer Key

Words are placed backwards, forward, diagonally, up and down. Words listed below are included in the maze. Circle the hidden vocabulary words in the maze.

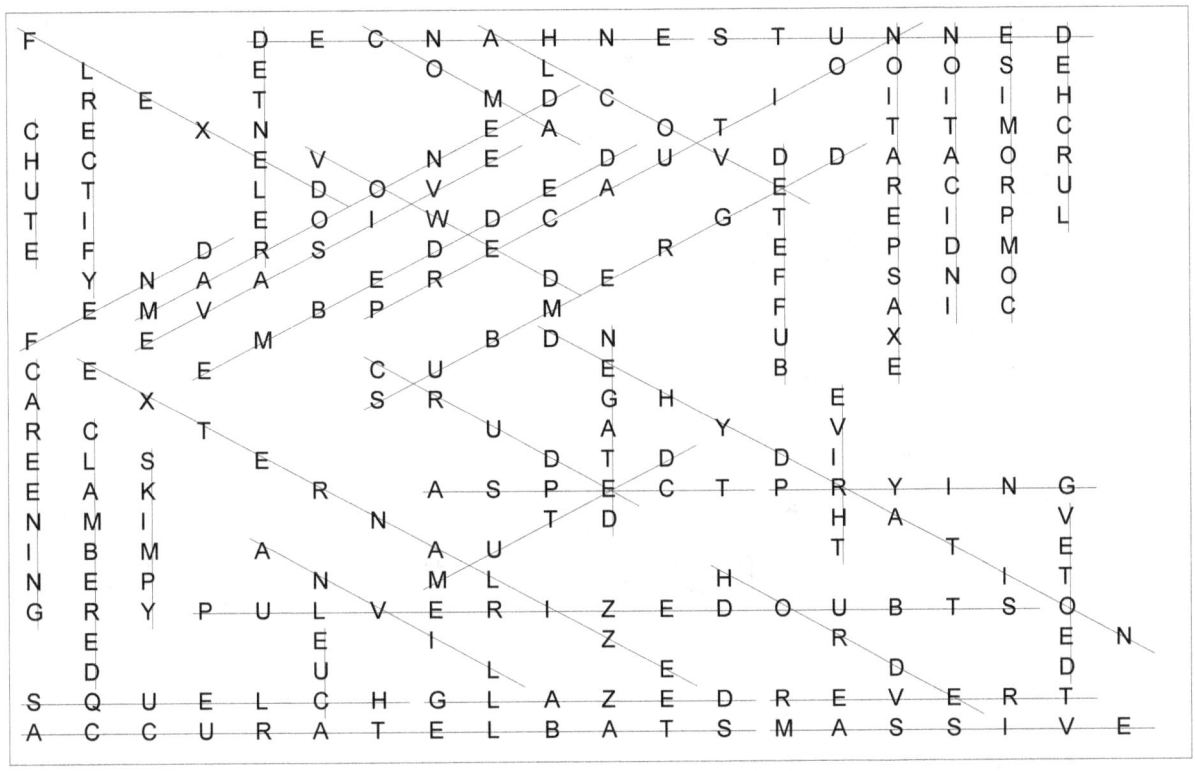

| ACCURATE | COMPROMISE | EXTERNALIZE | MUTED | SQUELCH |
| ALCOVE | CRUDE | FEND | NEGATED | STABLE |
| ANVIL | CUE | FLEXED | PRECAUTION | STUNNED |
| ASPECT | DEHYDRATION | GLAZED | PRYING | SUBMERGED |
| BUFFETED | DOUBTS | HORDE | PULVERIZED | THRIVE |
| CAREENING | EMBEDDED | INDICATION | RECTIFY | VETOED |
| CHUTE | ENHANCED | LURCHED | RELENTED | VOWED |
| CLAMBERED | EVASIVE | MAROONED | REVERT | |
| COMA | EXASPERATION | MASSIVE | SKIMPY | |

River Vocabulary Crossword 1

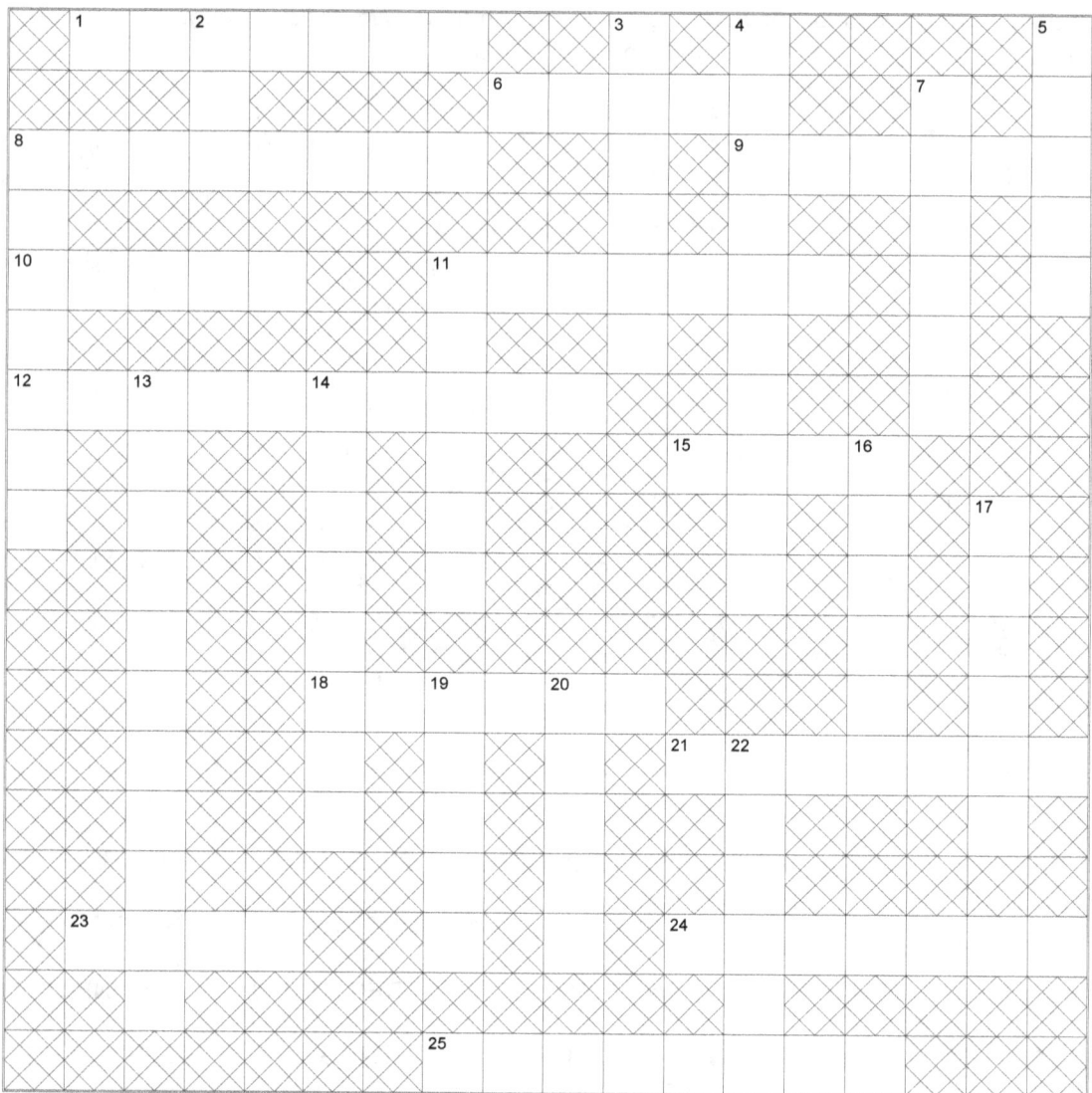

Across
1. To set right; correct
6. A large group; swarm
8. Firmly enclosed
9. To return to a former condition
10. Heavy block of iron or steel
11. Shocked
12. Sign; signal
15. Fight against
18. An indentation or small hollow
21. Enormous
23. Unconsciousness
24. Ruled out
25. Hit; beat

Down
2. Sign
3. Looking curiously; snooping
4. Wrongly stubborn
5. Muffled; softened
7. Rejected; refused
8. Misleading; avoiding
11. Not enough; inadequate
13. Loss of water or moisture
14. Exact
16. Uncertainties
17. Succeed
19. A waterfall; a channel
20. Promised
22. Way of looking at something

River Vocabulary Crossword 1 Answer Key

|   | 1 R | 2 E | C | T | I | F | Y |   | 3 P |   | 4 P |   |   | 7 V |   | 5 M |
|---|---|---|---|---|---|---|---|---|---|---|---|---|---|---|---|---|
|   |   | U |   |   |   |   |   | 6 H | O | R | D | E |   | V |   | U |
| 8 E | M | B | E | D | D | E | D |   | Y |   | 9 R | E | V | E | R | T |
| V |   |   |   |   |   |   |   |   | I |   | V |   |   | T |   | E |
| 10 A | N | V | I | L |   |   | 11 S | T | U | N | N | E | D |   | O |   | D |
| S |   |   |   |   |   |   | K |   | G |   | R |   |   | E |   |   |
| 12 I | N | 13 D | I | 14 C | A | T | I | O | N |   | S |   | 16 D |   |   |   |
| V |   | E |   | C |   |   | M |   |   | 15 F | E | N | D |   |   |   |
| E |   | H |   | C |   |   | P |   |   | L |   |   | O |   | 17 T |   |
|   |   | Y |   | U |   |   | Y |   |   | Y |   |   | U |   | H |   |
|   |   | D |   | R |   |   |   |   |   |   |   |   | B |   | R |   |
|   |   | R |   | 18 A | L | 19 C | O | 20 V | E |   |   |   | T |   | I |   |
|   |   | A |   | T |   | H |   | O |   | 21 M | 22 A | S | S | I | V | E |
|   |   | T |   | E |   | U |   | W |   |   | S |   |   |   | E |   |
|   |   | I |   |   |   | T |   | E |   |   | S |   |   |   |   |   |
|   |   | 23 C | O | M | A |   |   | E |   | 24 N | E | G | A | T | E | D |
|   |   | N |   |   |   |   |   | D |   |   | C |   |   |   |   |   |
|   |   |   |   | 25 B | U | F | F | E | T | E | D |   |   |   |   |   |

Across
1. To set right; correct
6. A large group; swarm
8. Firmly enclosed
9. To return to a former condition
10. Heavy block of iron or steel
11. Shocked
12. Sign; signal
15. Fight against
18. An indentation or small hollow
21. Enormous
23. Unconsciousness
24. Ruled out
25. Hit; beat

Down
2. Sign
3. Looking curiously; snooping
4. Wrongly stubborn
5. Muffled; softened
7. Rejected; refused
8. Misleading; avoiding
11. Not enough; inadequate
13. Loss of water or moisture
14. Exact
16. Uncertainties
17. Succeed
19. A waterfall; a channel
20. Promised
22. Way of looking at something

River Vocabulary Crossword 2

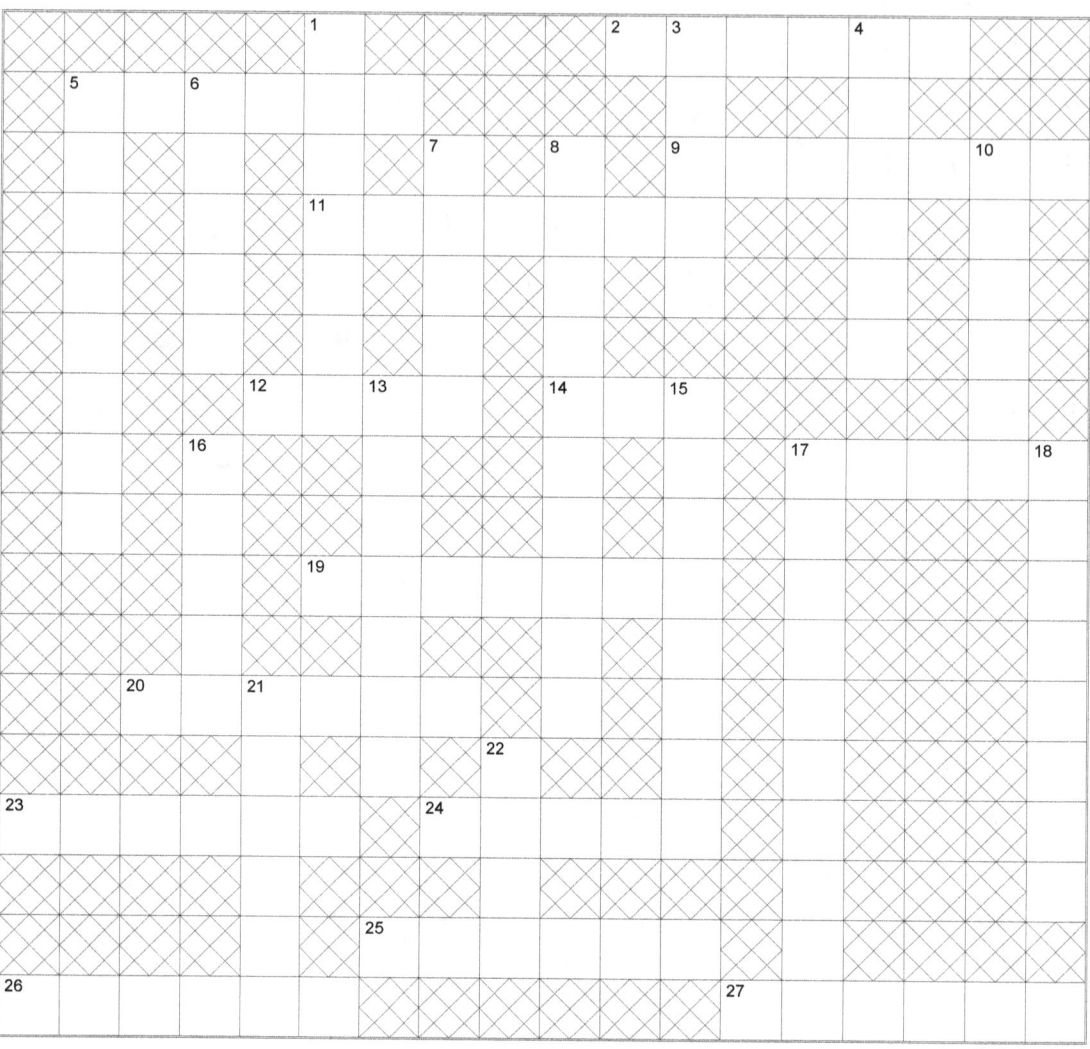

Across
2. Succeed
5. An indentation or small hollow
9. To set right; correct
11. Shocked
12. Fight against
14. Sign
17. Roughly made
19. Enormous
20. Glassy-eyed
23. Not enough; inadequate
24. Promised
25. Sturdy
26. Uncertainties
27. To return to a former condition

Down
1. Misleading; avoiding
3. A large group; swarm
4. Rejected; refused
5. Exact
6. A waterfall; a channel
7. Muffled; softened
8. Sign; signal
10. Bent
13. Ruled out
15. Firmly enclosed
16. Heavy block of iron or steel
17. Agreement
18. Improved
21. Way of looking at something
22. Unconsciousness

# River Vocabulary Crossword 2 Answer Key

|   |   |   | 1 E |   |   | 2 T | 3 H | R | I | 4 V | E |   |   |
|---|---|---|---|---|---|---|---|---|---|---|---|---|---|
| 5 A | L | 6 C | O | V | E |   |   | O |   | E |   |   |   |
| C |   | H | A |   | 7 M |   | 8 I | 9 R | E | C | T | I | 10 F | Y |
| C |   | U | 11 S | T | U | N | N | E | D |   | O |   | L |   |
| U |   | T | I |   | T |   | D | E |   |   | E |   | E |   |
| R |   | E | V |   | E |   | I |   |   |   | D |   | X |   |
| A |   |   | 12 F | E | 13 N | D |   | 14 C | U | 15 E |   |   | E |   |
| T |   | 16 A |   |   | E |   |   | A |   | M |   | 17 C | R | U | 18 D | E |
| E |   | N |   |   | G |   |   | T |   | B |   | O |   |   |   | N |
|   |   | V |   | 19 M | A | S | S | I | V | E |   | M |   |   |   | H |
|   |   | I |   |   | T |   |   | O |   | D |   | P |   |   |   | A |
|   | 20 G | L | 21 A | Z | E | D |   | N |   | D |   | R |   |   |   | N |
|   |   |   | S |   | D |   | 22 C |   |   | E |   | O |   |   |   | C |
| 23 S | K | I | M | P | Y |   | 24 V | O | W | E | D |   | M |   |   | E |
|   |   |   | E |   |   |   | O |   |   |   |   |   | I |   |   | D |
|   |   |   | C |   | 25 S | T | A | B | L | E |   |   | S |   |   |   |
| 26 D | O | U | B | T | S |   |   |   |   |   | 27 R | E | V | E | R | T |

### Across
2. Succeed
5. An indentation or small hollow
9. To set right; correct
11. Shocked
12. Fight against
14. Sign
17. Roughly made
19. Enormous
20. Glassy-eyed
23. Not enough; inadequate
24. Promised
25. Sturdy
26. Uncertainties
27. To return to a former condition

### Down
1. Misleading; avoiding
3. A large group; swarm
4. Rejected; refused
5. Exact
6. A waterfall; a channel
7. Muffled; softened
8. Sign; signal
10. Bent
13. Ruled out
15. Firmly enclosed
16. Heavy block of iron or steel
17. Agreement
18. Improved
21. Way of looking at something
22. Unconsciousness

River Vocabulary Crossword 3

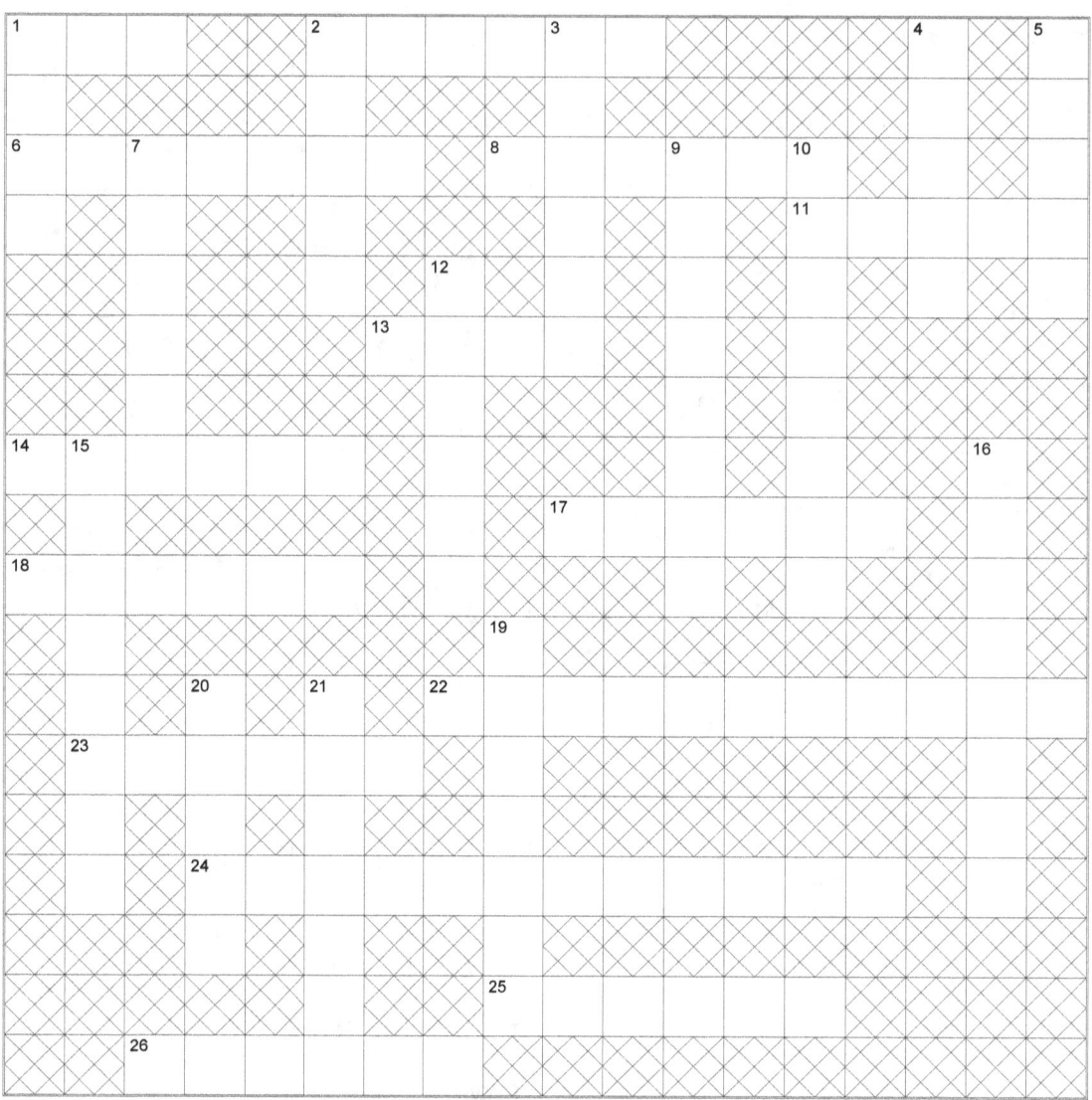

Across
1. Sign
2. An indentation or small hollow
6. Enormous
8. Sturdy
11. Muffled; softened
13. Fight against
14. Looking curiously; snooping
17. Bent
18. Glassy-eyed
22. Loss of water or moisture
23. Succeed
24. To fall apart
25. Uncertainties
26. Way of looking at something

Down
1. Unconsciousness
2. Heavy block of iron or steel
3. Rejected; refused
4. A waterfall; a channel
5. A large group; swarm
7. Not enough; inadequate
9. Hit; beat
10. Firmly enclosed
12. To return to a former condition
15. Eased off
16. Abandoned
19. Ruled out
20. Roughly made
21. Misleading; avoiding

# River Vocabulary Crossword 3 Answer Key

|   | 1 C | U | E |   | 2 A | L | C | O | V | E |   |   | 4 C |   | 5 H |
|---|---|---|---|---|---|---|---|---|---|---|---|---|---|---|---|
|   | O |   |   |   | N |   |   |   | E |   |   |   | H |   | O |
| 6 M | A | 7 S | S | I | V | E |   | 8 S | T | A | 9 B | 10 L | E |   | U | R |
|   | A |   | K |   | I |   |   |   | O |   | U |   | 11 M | U | T | E | D |
|   |   |   | I |   | L |   | 12 R | E |   | F |   | B |   | E |   | E |
|   |   |   | M |   |   | 13 F | E | N | D |   | F |   | E |   |   |   |
|   |   |   | P |   |   |   | V |   |   |   | E |   | D |   |   |   |
| 14 P | 15 R | Y | I | N | G |   | E |   |   | 17 F | T |   | D |   | 16 M |
|   | E |   |   |   |   |   | R |   | 17 F | L | E | X | E | D | A |
| 18 G | L | A | Z | E | D |   | T |   |   |   | D |   | D |   | R |
|   | E |   |   |   |   | 19 N |   |   |   |   |   |   |   |   | O |
|   | N |   | 20 C |   | 21 E |   | 22 D | E | H | Y | D | R | A | T | I | O | N |
|   | 23 T | H | R | I | V | E |   | G |   |   |   |   |   |   | N |
|   | E |   | U |   | A |   |   | A |   |   |   |   |   |   | E |
|   | D |   | 24 D | I | S | I | N | T | E | G | R | A | T | E | D |
|   |   |   | E |   | I |   |   | E |   |   |   |   |   |   |   |
|   |   |   |   |   | V |   |   | 25 D | O | U | B | T | S |   |   |
|   |   |   | 26 A | S | P | E | C | T |   |   |   |   |   |   |   |

Across
1. Sign
2. An indentation or small hollow
6. Enormous
8. Sturdy
11. Muffled; softened
13. Fight against
14. Looking curiously; snooping
17. Bent
18. Glassy-eyed
22. Loss of water or moisture
23. Succeed
24. To fall apart
25. Uncertainties
26. Way of looking at something

Down
1. Unconsciousness
2. Heavy block of iron or steel
3. Rejected; refused
4. A waterfall; a channel
5. A large group; swarm
7. Not enough; inadequate
9. Hit; beat
10. Firmly enclosed
12. To return to a former condition
15. Eased off
16. Abandoned
19. Ruled out
20. Roughly made
21. Misleading; avoiding

River Vocabulary Crossword 4

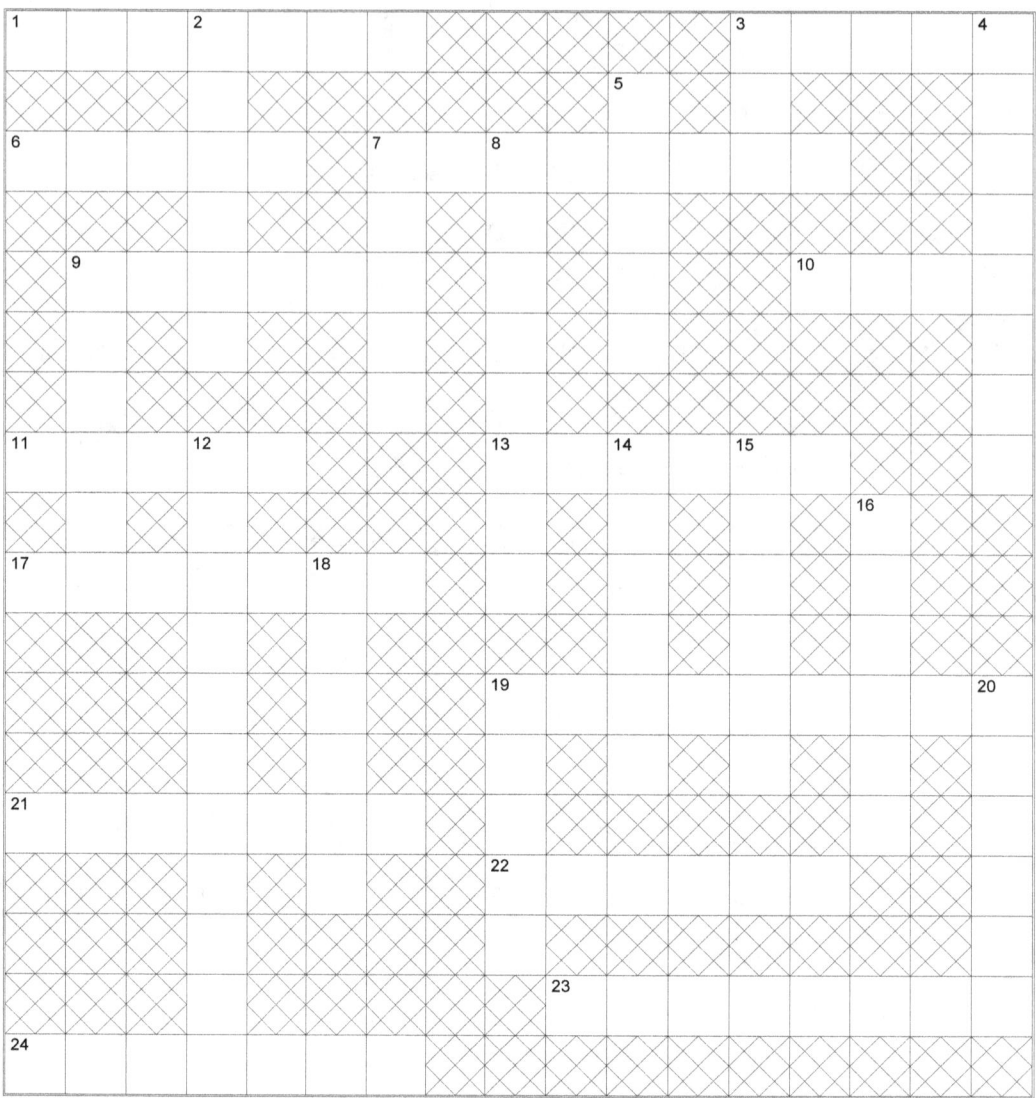

Across
1. Enormous
3. A waterfall; a channel
6. Heavy block of iron or steel
7. Abandoned
9. Way of looking at something
10. Fight against
11. Promised
13. Succeed
17. To set right; correct
19. Rushing headlong
21. Ruled out
22. Uncertainties
23. Improved
24. To silence

Down
2. Not enough; inadequate
3. Sign
4. Firmly enclosed
5. A large group; swarm
7. Muffled; softened
8. Eased off
9. An indentation or small hollow
12. To show outwardly
14. To return to a former condition
15. Rejected; refused
16. Looking curiously; snooping
18. Bent
19. Roughly made
20. Glassy-eyed

River Vocabulary Crossword 4 Answer Key

|   | 1 M | A | S | 2 S | I | V | E |   |   |   | 3 C | H | U | T | 4 E |
|---|---|---|---|---|---|---|---|---|---|---|---|---|---|---|---|
|   |   |   |   | K |   |   |   |   |   | 5 H |   | U |   |   | M |
|   | 6 A | N | V | I | L |   | 7 M | 8 A | R | O | O | N | E | D |   | B |
|   |   |   |   | M |   |   | U |   | E |   | R |   |   |   |   | E |
|   |   |   | 9 A | S | P | E | C | T |   | L |   | D |   | 10 F | E | N | D |
|   |   |   | L |   | Y |   |   | E |   | E |   | E |   |   |   |   | D |
|   |   |   | C |   |   |   | D |   | N |   |   |   |   |   |   | E |
|   | 11 V | O | W | 12 E | D |   |   | 13 T | H | 14 R | I | 15 V | E |   |   | D |
|   |   |   |   | V |   | X |   |   | E |   | E |   | E |   | 16 P |   |
|   | 17 R | E | C | T | I | 18 F | Y |   | D |   | V |   | T |   | R |   |
|   |   |   |   | E |   | L |   |   |   |   | E |   | O |   | Y |   |
|   |   |   |   | R |   | E |   | 19 C | A | R | E | E | N | I | N | 20 G |
|   |   |   |   | N |   | X |   | R |   | T |   |   | D |   | N |   | L |
|   | 21 N | E | G | A | T | E | D |   | 22 D | O | U | B | T | S |   | A |
|   |   |   |   | L |   | D |   |   |   |   |   |   |   | G |   | Z |
|   |   |   |   | I |   |   |   |   | E |   |   |   |   |   | E |
|   |   |   |   |   |   |   |   | 23 E | N | H | A | N | C | E | D |
|   | 24 S | Q | U | E | L | C | H |   |   |   |   |   |   |   |   |

Across
1. Enormous
3. A waterfall; a channel
6. Heavy block of iron or steel
7. Abandoned
9. Way of looking at something
10. Fight against
11. Promised
13. Succeed
17. To set right; correct
19. Rushing headlong
21. Ruled out
22. Uncertainties
23. Improved
24. To silence

Down
2. Not enough; inadequate
3. Sign
4. Firmly enclosed
5. A large group; swarm
7. Muffled; softened
8. Eased off
9. An indentation or small hollow
12. To show outwardly
14. To return to a former condition
15. Rejected; refused
16. Looking curiously; snooping
18. Bent
19. Roughly made
20. Glassy-eyed

River Vocabulary Juggle Letters 1

1. EDVTOE = 1. _____
   Rejected; refused

2. YPINRG = 2. _____
   Looking curiously; snooping

3. OAELCV = 3. _____
   An indentation or small hollow

4. MISPKY = 4. _____
   Not enough; inadequate

5. EDURC = 5. _____
   Roughly made

6. THCEU = 6. _____
   A waterfall; a channel

7. UCE = 7. _____
   Sign

8. ENDF = 8. _____
   Fight against

9. EBLTAS = 9. _____
   Sturdy

10. UILREPZVDE = 10. _____
    Ground to powder or dust

11. ERDOH = 11. _____
    A large group; swarm

12. LVERSEYREP = 12. _____
    Wrongly stubborn

13. IOECATPURN = 13. _____
    Safeguard

14. GREBMEUDS = 14. _____
    Covered with water

15. EUHQSLC = 15. _____
    To silence

River Vocabulary Juggle Letters 1 Answer Key

1. EDVTOE = 1. VETOED
Rejected; refused

2. YPINRG = 2. PRYING
Looking curiously; snooping

3. OAELCV = 3. ALCOVE
An indentation or small hollow

4. MISPKY = 4. SKIMPY
Not enough; inadequate

5. EDURC = 5. CRUDE
Roughly made

6. THCEU = 6. CHUTE
A waterfall; a channel

7. UCE = 7. CUE
Sign

8. ENDF = 8. FEND
Fight against

9. EBLTAS = 9. STABLE
Sturdy

10. UILREPZVDE = 10. PULVERIZED
Ground to powder or dust

11. ERDOH = 11. HORDE
A large group; swarm

12. LVERSEYREP = 12. PERVERSELY
Wrongly stubborn

13. IOECATPURN = 13. PRECAUTION
Safeguard

14. GREBMEUDS = 14. SUBMERGED
Covered with water

15. EUHQSLC = 15. SQUELCH
To silence

Copyrighted

River Vocabulary Juggle Letters 2

1. ELSATB = 1. _____
   Sturdy

2. VEAMSIS = 2. _____
   Enormous

3. ETPCSA = 3. _____
   Way of looking at something

4. EDCRU = 4. _____
   Roughly made

5. OVEETD = 5. _____
   Rejected; refused

6. EWDOV = 6. _____
   Promised

7. UHEDLCR = 7. _____
   Rolled; dipped down

8. RNEAIELTXEZ = 8. _____
   To show outwardly

9. UTNNSED = 9. _____
   Shocked

10. EREVTR = 10. _____
    To return to a former condition

11. BDOTUS = 11. _____
    Uncertainties

12. UTEHC = 12. _____
    A waterfall; a channel

13. ISOORPEMCM = 13. _____
    Agreement

14. FTUDEBFE = 14. _____
    Hit; beat

15. USQLCEH = 15. _____
    To silence

River Vocabulary Juggle Letters 2 Answer Key

1. ELSATB = 1. STABLE
Sturdy

2. VEAMSIS = 2. MASSIVE
Enormous

3. ETPCSA = 3. ASPECT
Way of looking at something

4. EDCRU = 4. CRUDE
Roughly made

5. OVEETD = 5. VETOED
Rejected; refused

6. EWDOV = 6. VOWED
Promised

7. UHEDLCR = 7. LURCHED
Rolled; dipped down

8. RNEAIELTXEZ = 8. EXTERNALIZE
To show outwardly

9. UTNNSED = 9. STUNNED
Shocked

10. EREVTR = 10. REVERT
To return to a former condition

11. BDOTUS = 11. DOUBTS
Uncertainties

12. UTEHC = 12. CHUTE
A waterfall; a channel

13. ISOORPEMCM = 13. COMPROMISE
Agreement

14. FTUDEBFE = 14. BUFFETED
Hit; beat

15. USQLCEH = 15. SQUELCH
To silence

River Vocabulary Juggle Letters 3

1. GNRCEAIEN = 1. _____
   Rushing headlong

2. TGTERENIDASI = 2. _____
   To fall apart

3. ECAPTS = 3. _____
   Way of looking at something

4. MSROOEIPCM = 4. _____
   Agreement

5. LTSBAE = 5. _____
   Sturdy

6. XDEELF = 6. _____
   Bent

7. VREHIT = 7. _____
   Succeed

8. DNETLEER = 8. _____
   Eased off

9. TRVREE = 9. _____
   To return to a former condition

10. ELRNXZETIAE =10. _____
    To show outwardly

11. CEVAOL =11. _____
    An indentation or small hollow

12. UCE =12. _____
    Sign

13. TYRFIEC =13. _____
    To set right; correct

14. RLEDUCH =14. _____
    Rolled; dipped down

15. ECAAUTRC =15. _____
    Exact

River Vocabulary Juggle Letters 3 Answer Key

1. GNRCEAIEN = 1. CAREENING
Rushing headlong

2. TGTERENIDASI = 2. DISINTEGRATE
To fall apart

3. ECAPTS = 3. ASPECT
Way of looking at something

4. MSROOEIPCM = 4. COMPROMISE
Agreement

5. LTSBAE = 5. STABLE
Sturdy

6. XDEELF = 6. FLEXED
Bent

7. VREHIT = 7. THRIVE
Succeed

8. DNETLEER = 8. RELENTED
Eased off

9. TRVREE = 9. REVERT
To return to a former condition

10. ELRNXZETIAE = 10. EXTERNALIZE
To show outwardly

11. CEVAOL = 11. ALCOVE
An indentation or small hollow

12. UCE = 12. CUE
Sign

13. TYRFIEC = 13. RECTIFY
To set right; correct

14. RLEDUCH = 14. LURCHED
Rolled; dipped down

15. ECAAUTRC = 15. ACCURATE
Exact

River Vocabulary Juggle Letters 4

1. GNERNCEIA = 1. _____
   Rushing headlong

2. UCE = 2. _____
   Sign

3. TEALBS = 3. _____
   Sturdy

4. AOCM = 4. _____
   Unconsciousness

5. IFTECRY = 5. _____
   To set right; correct

6. ZLERUIDVEP = 6. _____
   Ground to powder or dust

7. AILVN = 7. _____
   Heavy block of iron or steel

8. GADTEEN = 8. _____
   Ruled out

9. BSODTU = 9. _____
   Uncertainties

10. ETUMD = 10. _____
    Muffled; softened

11. AETUARCC = 11. _____
    Exact

12. DHOAEYINTDR = 12. _____
    Loss of water or moisture

13. IAPUEORNTC = 13. _____
    Safeguard

14. NXETIEZAREL = 14. _____
    To show outwardly

15. RTGIASNEDTIE = 15. _____
    To fall apart

River Vocabulary Juggle Letters 4 Answer Key

1. GNERNCEIA = 1. CAREENING
   Rushing headlong

2. UCE = 2. CUE
   Sign

3. TEALBS = 3. STABLE
   Sturdy

4. AOCM = 4. COMA
   Unconsciousness

5. IFTECRY = 5. RECTIFY
   To set right; correct

6. ZLERUIDVEP = 6. PULVERIZED
   Ground to powder or dust

7. AILVN = 7. ANVIL
   Heavy block of iron or steel

8. GADTEEN = 8. NEGATED
   Ruled out

9. BSODTU = 9. DOUBTS
   Uncertainties

10. ETUMD = 10. MUTED
    Muffled; softened

11. AETUARCC = 11. ACCURATE
    Exact

12. DHOAEYINTDR = 12. DEHYDRATION
    Loss of water or moisture

13. IAPUEORNTC = 13. PRECAUTION
    Safeguard

14. NXETIEZAREL = 14. EXTERNALIZE
    To show outwardly

15. RTGIASNEDTIE = 15. DISINTEGRATE
    To fall apart

| | |
|---|---|
| ACCURATE | Exact |
| ALCOVE | An indentation or small hollow |
| ANVIL | Heavy block of iron or steel |
| ASPECT | Way of looking at something |
| BUFFETED | Hit; beat |
| CAREENING | Rushing headlong |

| | |
|---|---|
| CHUTE | A waterfall; a channel |
| CLAMBERED | Climbed |
| COMA | Unconsciousness |
| COMPROMISE | Agreement |
| CRUDE | Roughly made |
| CUE | Sign |

| | |
|---|---|
| DEHYDRATION | Loss of water or moisture |
| DISINTEGRATE | To fall apart |
| DOUBTS | Uncertainties |
| EMBEDDED | Firmly enclosed |
| ENHANCED | Improved |
| EVASIVE | Misleading; avoiding |

| | |
|---|---|
| EXASPERATION | Annoyance |
| EXTERNALIZE | To show outwardly |
| FEND | Fight against |
| FLEXED | Bent |
| GLAZED | Glassy-eyed |
| HORDE | A large group; swarm |

| | |
|---|---|
| INDICATION | Sign; signal |
| LURCHED | Rolled; dipped down |
| MAROONED | Abandoned |
| MASSIVE | Enormous |
| MUTED | Muffled; softened |
| NEGATED | Ruled out |

| | |
|---|---|
| PERVERSELY | Wrongly stubborn |
| PRECAUTION | Safeguard |
| PRYING | Looking curiously; snooping |
| PULVERIZED | Ground to powder or dust |
| RECTIFY | To set right; correct |
| RELENTED | Eased off |

| REVERT | To return to a former condition |
|---|---|
| SKIMPY | Not enough; inadequate |
| SQUELCH | To silence |
| STABLE | Sturdy |
| STUNNED | Shocked |
| SUBMERGED | Covered with water |

| | |
|---|---|
| THRIVE | Succeed |
| VETOED | Rejected; refused |
| VOWED | Promised |

River Vocabulary

| PERVERSELY | CAREENING | CUE | ASPECT | RELENTED |
|---|---|---|---|---|
| MAROONED | CLAMBERED | SUBMERGED | GLAZED | EXTERNALIZE |
| THRIVE | COMA | FREE SPACE | DISINTEGRATE | ENHANCED |
| STUNNED | ALCOVE | DOUBTS | PRECAUTION | EXASPERATION |
| PULVERIZED | VOWED | STABLE | FEND | SQUELCH |

River Vocabulary

| PRYING | FLEXED | MASSIVE | MUTED | COMPROMISE |
|---|---|---|---|---|
| LURCHED | VETOED | CHUTE | DEHYDRATION | HORDE |
| RECTIFY | CRUDE | FREE SPACE | ACCURATE | NEGATED |
| EMBEDDED | EVASIVE | SKIMPY | REVERT | BUFFETED |
| SQUELCH | FEND | STABLE | VOWED | PULVERIZED |

River Vocabulary

| ASPECT | COMA | EVASIVE | STUNNED | DOUBTS |
|---|---|---|---|---|
| PRYING | ENHANCED | CHUTE | MAROONED | RECTIFY |
| PERVERSELY | INDICATION | FREE SPACE | LURCHED | COMPROMISE |
| EXTERNALIZE | EXASPERATION | STABLE | VETOED | THRIVE |
| DISINTEGRATE | SQUELCH | GLAZED | PULVERIZED | REVERT |

River Vocabulary

| BUFFETED | HORDE | VOWED | MASSIVE | CRUDE |
|---|---|---|---|---|
| CLAMBERED | CAREENING | SUBMERGED | ANVIL | ALCOVE |
| FEND | CUE | FREE SPACE | RELENTED | PRECAUTION |
| SKIMPY | EMBEDDED | FLEXED | NEGATED | ACCURATE |
| REVERT | PULVERIZED | GLAZED | SQUELCH | DISINTEGRATE |

## River Vocabulary

| VOWED | STABLE | SUBMERGED | ACCURATE | MASSIVE |
|---|---|---|---|---|
| GLAZED | CRUDE | EXASPERATION | BUFFETED | RECTIFY |
| FLEXED | RELENTED | FREE SPACE | EMBEDDED | DISINTEGRATE |
| CHUTE | CUE | VETOED | REVERT | ENHANCED |
| ANVIL | MUTED | ASPECT | COMA | EXTERNALIZE |

## River Vocabulary

| NEGATED | INDICATION | STUNNED | PRYING | MAROONED |
|---|---|---|---|---|
| COMPROMISE | HORDE | THRIVE | PULVERIZED | LURCHED |
| EVASIVE | SKIMPY | FREE SPACE | DOUBTS | ALCOVE |
| PRECAUTION | DEHYDRATION | CAREENING | CLAMBERED | PERVERSELY |
| EXTERNALIZE | COMA | ASPECT | MUTED | ANVIL |

River Vocabulary

| MAROONED | STABLE | CRUDE | THRIVE | VOWED |
|---|---|---|---|---|
| FEND | RECTIFY | SUBMERGED | LURCHED | PRYING |
| COMPROMISE | ANVIL | FREE SPACE | EXTERNALIZE | ACCURATE |
| EXASPERATION | PULVERIZED | DISINTEGRATE | ASPECT | DOUBTS |
| PRECAUTION | PERVERSELY | NEGATED | SKIMPY | FLEXED |

River Vocabulary

| SQUELCH | CHUTE | EMBEDDED | CAREENING | INDICATION |
|---|---|---|---|---|
| CUE | ALCOVE | HORDE | STUNNED | MASSIVE |
| REVERT | BUFFETED | FREE SPACE | ENHANCED | DEHYDRATION |
| VETOED | CLAMBERED | COMA | RELENTED | GLAZED |
| FLEXED | SKIMPY | NEGATED | PERVERSELY | PRECAUTION |

## River Vocabulary

| RELENTED | PULVERIZED | REVERT | COMPROMISE | SKIMPY |
|---|---|---|---|---|
| EMBEDDED | FEND | BUFFETED | PRECAUTION | NEGATED |
| INDICATION | DOUBTS | FREE SPACE | GLAZED | ANVIL |
| EXASPERATION | VOWED | PERVERSELY | ACCURATE | EXTERNALIZE |
| DISINTEGRATE | STUNNED | ENHANCED | MUTED | CRUDE |

## River Vocabulary

| SQUELCH | CHUTE | RECTIFY | HORDE | THRIVE |
|---|---|---|---|---|
| CAREENING | ASPECT | MASSIVE | VETOED | CLAMBERED |
| STABLE | COMA | FREE SPACE | LURCHED | SUBMERGED |
| PRYING | MAROONED | ALCOVE | FLEXED | DEHYDRATION |
| CRUDE | MUTED | ENHANCED | STUNNED | DISINTEGRATE |

## River Vocabulary

| ALCOVE | STUNNED | ACCURATE | THRIVE | HORDE |
|---|---|---|---|---|
| CAREENING | PRECAUTION | PRYING | RECTIFY | COMPROMISE |
| REVERT | CUE | FREE SPACE | STABLE | MASSIVE |
| SUBMERGED | PERVERSELY | RELENTED | VOWED | SKIMPY |
| VETOED | FEND | PULVERIZED | BUFFETED | COMA |

## River Vocabulary

| CLAMBERED | EMBEDDED | MAROONED | ENHANCED | EXASPERATION |
|---|---|---|---|---|
| DOUBTS | DEHYDRATION | LURCHED | EVASIVE | GLAZED |
| ASPECT | SQUELCH | FREE SPACE | FLEXED | NEGATED |
| CRUDE | ANVIL | EXTERNALIZE | DISINTEGRATE | INDICATION |
| COMA | BUFFETED | PULVERIZED | FEND | VETOED |

River Vocabulary

| PRYING | GLAZED | FEND | DISINTEGRATE | CLAMBERED |
|---|---|---|---|---|
| VOWED | THRIVE | MUTED | ANVIL | PRECAUTION |
| FLEXED | HORDE | FREE SPACE | ALCOVE | COMA |
| MASSIVE | COMPROMISE | EXASPERATION | DEHYDRATION | VETOED |
| CUE | EVASIVE | DOUBTS | RELENTED | SUBMERGED |

River Vocabulary

| ENHANCED | SKIMPY | CHUTE | REVERT | BUFFETED |
|---|---|---|---|---|
| PERVERSELY | ACCURATE | STABLE | PULVERIZED | MAROONED |
| NEGATED | CRUDE | FREE SPACE | SQUELCH | RECTIFY |
| EXTERNALIZE | ASPECT | STUNNED | INDICATION | EMBEDDED |
| SUBMERGED | RELENTED | DOUBTS | EVASIVE | CUE |

River Vocabulary

| ENHANCED | EXTERNALIZE | EXASPERATION | RELENTED | CLAMBERED |
|---|---|---|---|---|
| MASSIVE | PULVERIZED | FEND | BUFFETED | NEGATED |
| COMPROMISE | INDICATION | FREE SPACE | LURCHED | MUTED |
| THRIVE | STUNNED | PERVERSELY | CAREENING | ACCURATE |
| ASPECT | EMBEDDED | DISINTEGRATE | SQUELCH | COMA |

River Vocabulary

| DEHYDRATION | VETOED | CHUTE | RECTIFY | FLEXED |
|---|---|---|---|---|
| VOWED | PRECAUTION | MAROONED | PRYING | REVERT |
| EVASIVE | CRUDE | FREE SPACE | SUBMERGED | STABLE |
| ANVIL | CUE | HORDE | SKIMPY | DOUBTS |
| COMA | SQUELCH | DISINTEGRATE | EMBEDDED | ASPECT |

River Vocabulary

| VOWED | DEHYDRATION | ASPECT | COMPROMISE | LURCHED |
|---|---|---|---|---|
| PRYING | CAREENING | PERVERSELY | CUE | ALCOVE |
| INDICATION | ENHANCED | FREE SPACE | PRECAUTION | FLEXED |
| SUBMERGED | SQUELCH | HORDE | REVERT | MUTED |
| STABLE | VETOED | RELENTED | PULVERIZED | COMA |

River Vocabulary

| MAROONED | ANVIL | DOUBTS | EXASPERATION | THRIVE |
|---|---|---|---|---|
| GLAZED | SKIMPY | EXTERNALIZE | STUNNED | CLAMBERED |
| NEGATED | CHUTE | FREE SPACE | BUFFETED | ACCURATE |
| MASSIVE | EVASIVE | CRUDE | RECTIFY | DISINTEGRATE |
| COMA | PULVERIZED | RELENTED | VETOED | STABLE |

River Vocabulary

| DEHYDRATION | HORDE | ALCOVE | REVERT | DISINTEGRATE |
|---|---|---|---|---|
| EXTERNALIZE | MUTED | SQUELCH | SUBMERGED | CHUTE |
| STUNNED | PERVERSELY | FREE SPACE | VETOED | EMBEDDED |
| EVASIVE | LURCHED | EXASPERATION | ACCURATE | MAROONED |
| FLEXED | THRIVE | ASPECT | MASSIVE | PRECAUTION |

River Vocabulary

| BUFFETED | SKIMPY | FEND | NEGATED | PULVERIZED |
|---|---|---|---|---|
| DOUBTS | COMA | ANVIL | INDICATION | GLAZED |
| CLAMBERED | RECTIFY | FREE SPACE | CUE | CAREENING |
| STABLE | PRYING | COMPROMISE | CRUDE | RELENTED |
| PRECAUTION | MASSIVE | ASPECT | THRIVE | FLEXED |

River Vocabulary

| SQUELCH | INDICATION | MUTED | DISINTEGRATE | NEGATED |
|---|---|---|---|---|
| SUBMERGED | STUNNED | CRUDE | EXTERNALIZE | RELENTED |
| ANVIL | VETOED | FREE SPACE | ALCOVE | PERVERSELY |
| CHUTE | FLEXED | COMA | PRECAUTION | HORDE |
| PULVERIZED | RECTIFY | CLAMBERED | CAREENING | DOUBTS |

River Vocabulary

| GLAZED | ENHANCED | EVASIVE | ACCURATE | VOWED |
|---|---|---|---|---|
| MAROONED | MASSIVE | LURCHED | COMPROMISE | THRIVE |
| REVERT | DEHYDRATION | FREE SPACE | STABLE | EMBEDDED |
| SKIMPY | EXASPERATION | FEND | CUE | BUFFETED |
| DOUBTS | CAREENING | CLAMBERED | RECTIFY | PULVERIZED |

River Vocabulary

| PULVERIZED | THRIVE | INDICATION | BUFFETED | GLAZED |
| --- | --- | --- | --- | --- |
| SUBMERGED | FLEXED | EVASIVE | PRECAUTION | CAREENING |
| EXTERNALIZE | ANVIL | FREE SPACE | LURCHED | COMPROMISE |
| CRUDE | CUE | PRYING | CHUTE | MASSIVE |
| DISINTEGRATE | STABLE | ASPECT | SQUELCH | ENHANCED |

River Vocabulary

| MAROONED | VOWED | VETOED | EMBEDDED | RECTIFY |
| --- | --- | --- | --- | --- |
| DEHYDRATION | FEND | ALCOVE | COMA | HORDE |
| PERVERSELY | DOUBTS | FREE SPACE | STUNNED | NEGATED |
| REVERT | MUTED | EXASPERATION | SKIMPY | RELENTED |
| ENHANCED | SQUELCH | ASPECT | STABLE | DISINTEGRATE |

River Vocabulary

| INDICATION | BUFFETED | COMPROMISE | FEND | CUE |
|---|---|---|---|---|
| PRYING | VETOED | NEGATED | STUNNED | MASSIVE |
| EXASPERATION | MUTED | FREE SPACE | PERVERSELY | EMBEDDED |
| RECTIFY | REVERT | PRECAUTION | ALCOVE | THRIVE |
| LURCHED | COMA | SUBMERGED | CHUTE | VOWED |

River Vocabulary

| MAROONED | CLAMBERED | ACCURATE | ENHANCED | ANVIL |
|---|---|---|---|---|
| EVASIVE | PULVERIZED | DISINTEGRATE | CRUDE | EXTERNALIZE |
| FLEXED | GLAZED | FREE SPACE | DOUBTS | DEHYDRATION |
| ASPECT | SQUELCH | HORDE | RELENTED | SKIMPY |
| VOWED | CHUTE | SUBMERGED | COMA | LURCHED |

River Vocabulary

| CUE | PULVERIZED | VOWED | INDICATION | EMBEDDED |
|---|---|---|---|---|
| HORDE | SKIMPY | CLAMBERED | MAROONED | MUTED |
| CRUDE | PERVERSELY | FREE SPACE | COMPROMISE | BUFFETED |
| ENHANCED | DOUBTS | COMA | STUNNED | ANVIL |
| STABLE | REVERT | CAREENING | NEGATED | ACCURATE |

River Vocabulary

| ASPECT | LURCHED | SUBMERGED | SQUELCH | CHUTE |
|---|---|---|---|---|
| FLEXED | DEHYDRATION | ALCOVE | MASSIVE | VETOED |
| EVASIVE | THRIVE | FREE SPACE | EXASPERATION | PRECAUTION |
| PRYING | RECTIFY | DISINTEGRATE | GLAZED | FEND |
| ACCURATE | NEGATED | CAREENING | REVERT | STABLE |

River Vocabulary

| ANVIL | MAROONED | LURCHED | PRYING | CRUDE |
|---|---|---|---|---|
| DEHYDRATION | CLAMBERED | DISINTEGRATE | PRECAUTION | NEGATED |
| FEND | SUBMERGED | FREE SPACE | EMBEDDED | RECTIFY |
| EXTERNALIZE | EXASPERATION | VOWED | RELENTED | SKIMPY |
| PERVERSELY | STABLE | CAREENING | GLAZED | EVASIVE |

River Vocabulary

| ENHANCED | COMPROMISE | ACCURATE | REVERT | CHUTE |
|---|---|---|---|---|
| STUNNED | ALCOVE | ASPECT | THRIVE | INDICATION |
| DOUBTS | SQUELCH | FREE SPACE | PULVERIZED | FLEXED |
| CUE | MASSIVE | BUFFETED | HORDE | VETOED |
| EVASIVE | GLAZED | CAREENING | STABLE | PERVERSELY |

River Vocabulary

| DEHYDRATION | STABLE | COMA | PRECAUTION | PULVERIZED |
|---|---|---|---|---|
| SUBMERGED | ALCOVE | RELENTED | CRUDE | FEND |
| DISINTEGRATE | LURCHED | FREE SPACE | FLEXED | SQUELCH |
| NEGATED | ENHANCED | DOUBTS | MUTED | EXASPERATION |
| ACCURATE | REVERT | EVASIVE | EXTERNALIZE | THRIVE |

River Vocabulary

| ASPECT | PRYING | CHUTE | CAREENING | RECTIFY |
|---|---|---|---|---|
| EMBEDDED | CLAMBERED | MASSIVE | MAROONED | VOWED |
| INDICATION | GLAZED | FREE SPACE | PERVERSELY | SKIMPY |
| BUFFETED | HORDE | COMPROMISE | ANVIL | CUE |
| THRIVE | EXTERNALIZE | EVASIVE | REVERT | ACCURATE |